moderneclectic

moderneclectic

orianna fielding banks

photography by michael banks

mitchell beazley

For Sasha

First published in Great Britain in 2001 by Mitchell Beazley, an imprint of
Octopus Publishing Group Limited, 2-4 Heron Quays, London E14 4JP

Project Editor: **Lara Maiklem**
Executive Art Editor: **Auberon Hedgecoe**
Editor: **Lisa Dyer**
Design: **Smith**
Production: **Angela Couchman**
Proof Reading and Index: **Kathleen M. Gill**

ISBN 1 84000 341 3

A CIP catalogue record for this book is available from the British Library

Typeset in Helvetica
Produced by Toppan Printing Co. (HK) Ltd.
Printed and bound in China

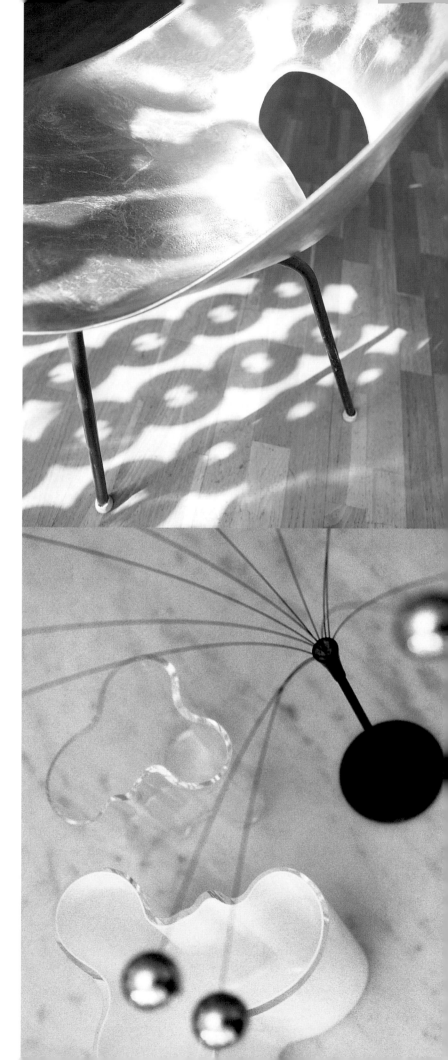

Contents

Introduction

odern eclecticism is about making interior design personal. A fusion of wit and whimsy, the modern eclectic movement holds a mesmeric fascination for both its creators and inhabitants because of its uniquely individual ethos. It is a platform from which to unleash the imagination, to explore the surreal, and to push the boundaries of convention. In breaking the traditional mores of design by challenging established expectations, it is the rogue gene of interior design and has the allure of all things uncategorizable.

As a movement, modern eclecticism has a refreshing freedom that is unhindered by the constraints of a particular "look" or "style" of the moment. It is an arena within which fashion and furniture can meld, scale can span the oversized to the overstated, and design can be expressed in theatrical broad sweeps or entrenched in minute detail. A multilayered, textural, and highly individual form of three-dimensional self-expression, modern eclecticism confidently combines the classic with the contemporary, the linear with the lustrous, the ornate with the organic, and the unexpected with the exotic. It is the ultimate fusion of the designed with the discovered – a place where opposites attract, and it encourages original thought and expression in the creation of a totally unique space.

Historically, eclecticism in interior design first surfaced as a movement in the early part of the 20th century, inspired by new forms of self-expression that were then being explored in the fields of art, theatre, and fashion. Toward the latter part of the century, in the 1990s, a new form of the movement emerged: modern eclecticism. It was born of a reaction to minimalism, in which interior environments

Left The marble fireplace is lit by coloured neon strip lights. Below, a classical Roman head, cast in clay, stands on the bronze-patinated hearth. Above a 1950s-inspired media cabinet by Orianna Fielding Banks hang two of Michael Banks' photo-art pieces.

Right The lounge was once used as a ballroom. The original pelmet, finished in gold leaf, follows the curve of the cornice. CDs are strung together to form reflective suspended panels and a walnut modular table, by Orianna Fielding Banks, stands on the right.

were deconstructed into planes, areas, surfaces, and finishes, forming a sometimes overly sterile arena within which the daily minutiae of life at times felt nomadic and displaced. Although the purity of lines and the sleekness of finishes in minimalism often provided a welcome stillness and an atmosphere of calm away from the daily stresses of urban living, the pressures of having to live an over-ordered life within an under-complicated interior inevitably led to an overwhelming desire to install a curve where a hard edge had been. Surfaces seemed to scream for pattern, white walls suddenly looked naked without colour, and smooth surfaces appeared strangely self-effacing without texture to give them substance.

The *fin de siècle* excesses, historically chronicled in fashion, theatre, art, and architecture, bring with them a kind of new bravado that is born of euphoric anticipation. The advent of a new century has historically been accompanied by a new confidence, a spirit of adventure, which is expressed at the end of the 20th century by a desire to break away from the confines of tradition. In modern eclecticism "out of context" is newly in vogue in an environment where the miscontextualization of key elements

Above Left Perched on the gold-leafed wooden shelf is a brushed aluminium frame, holding a green refractive postcard. The frame is one of a pair found in a fleamarket in Provence. The postcard refers back to curved references running throughout the space.

Left The original ceramic lamp base in latte tones of brown and beige is lit by a red bulb. It washes the media cabinet below it in a warm glow, building on the 1950s references. Next to the lamp stands a mirror mosaic vase and a "Leonardo" black vase.

creates a form of reverse cohesion, a space where eclecticism holds all the allure of a reluctant hero. Modern eclecticism provides the opportunity to explore the endless permutations that anarchic fusions of mixed disciplines, such as art with fashion, theatre with sculpture, or nature and history, can create. In doing so, it provides the same sense of excitement that discovering a new colour or texture holds for an artist or the exquisite satisfaction that achieving a perfectly perpendicular plane holds for an architect. For example, the juxtapositioning of an ornate 17th-century marble fireplace with a black-and-white block-mounted Bridget Riley print, hanging on a silver leaf wall and lit by a Verner Panton pendant light, has the ability to instil a deep sense of excitement and fulfilment in the creator of that space, capturing perfectly the essence of this new movement.

Modern eclecticism is a celebration of the cultural richness and diversity that surrounds us, providing an opportunity to translate international influences into a local context with pattern, texture, colour, shape, form, and surface – all awaiting individual interpretation. Driven by passion, pleasure, and personality, modern eclecticism does not follow design diktats or theorems; it is a nonconformist movement with no defining lead or direction, and that is its appeal. It is the ultimate form of self-expression and can be as transient or timeless, as understated or overwhelming, as simple or as self-indulgent, as desired. Modern eclecticism celebrates the "cult of the individual" and is ultimately about "doing your own edit." With its unique potential to transcend the boundaries of century, country, and culture, it offers an exceptional arena within which to create a uniquely personal interiorscape.

Below Standing on the veneered, burr ash "Alpi" coffee table by Orianna Fielding Banks is an original retro 1960s lamp with a spun plastic base and a Japanese vellum shade. Behind, the radiators have been painted in an old gold metallic paint to blend with the walls. Above, a circular twig decoration is mounted onto a gold-leafed baroque shelf like an organic art piece.

Colour

Colour is everywhere, permeating every aspect of our environment. Colour has an emotional language equal to that of music: it can provoke the deepest responses. In the same way that a note or musical phrase can transport us back to a treasured moment or lead us on an imaginary journey, so colour can dramatically affect our mood and impact the atmosphere of our surroundings.

In its modern eclectic manifestation, colour has a vital role to play. It has the ability to lend cohesion to a disparate palette of elements by providing continuity through different textures, forms, and surfaces, but it can also encourage chaos by reversing its established applications. Colour has the opportunity to "go solo" and become the vibrant focal point of an interior, either in paint form on walls, in floor coverings, on a signature piece of furniture, or by using coloured lighting. A single colour can highlight the key features of a space, providing a unifying element, or neighbouring tones of a limited palette can be explored in a dynamic form throughout an interior, in the same way that a musical theme reaffirms the underlying story line of a film.

Light is the partner of colour. Natural and artificial light will affect the way colours appear and will establish atmosphere. Natural daylight has its own colour palette, ranging from the cool, blue tones of a northern light to the warm, yellow-orange tones of a southern light. Colour can be used to enhance or counteract the inherent qualities of natural light, and light in turn can radically alter colour. Artificial lighting can now mimic the qualities of natural light, in warm tones with halogens, in yellow tones with traditional tungsten lighting, or in cool daylight shades with broad band fluorescents. Recent advances in technology have created products that merge colour with light. Originally developed for commercial applications, such as bars and clubs, these forms, Colourwash by Isometrix being one, are now available for residential interiors. Surfaces can be washed instantly with any colour from the spectrum at the touch of a button, transforming an interior into a technicoloured dreamscape. These adaptable light sources create the perfect arena in which to revel in the possibilities of a palette and to celebrate the contrasting personalities of colour.

Inspiration for a colour scheme can be triggered by a variety of external stimuli, from a piece of wrapping paper to the ornate gilding on a cathedral door to

Above Left The deep saturated colour of the cherry red, velvet armchair is highlighted by the fine stripes in midnight blue that separate the colour into broad bands. The armchair visually links the two separate living areas.

Above Right Light resting on the organic form of the blue Murano glass ashtray creates a secondary self-pattern. The intense tonal palette, spanning deepest charcoal to the softest sky blue, is reflected in the high-sheen Formica table.

Below Left A fuchsia-pink fluorescent strip light has been placed inside an oversized floor-standing wicker shade in a cone shape, creating an imaginative floor light that looks as if it has been threaded with neon.

Below Right Two transparent Perspex sheets hold a collection of red silk rose petals in a floor-standing light. The petals arrange themselves randomly, forming a textural screen that is backlit by a halogen bulb.

vibrantly coloured spices seen in a foreign marketplace. Anything observed by the senses can provide references for a colour scheme, turning a transient moment into a permanent decorative statement. As a tool, colour has the power to totally transform an interior and it is one of the most cost-effective ways to alter a space. A historical period can be replicated by using colours of that era, or this idea can be inverted by painting ornate historical architectural detailing in vibrant contemporary hues. Colour is an ideal medium to use to visually alter the proportions of a room by applying light and dark tones on strategic planes. A generic space can be transformed into a soft, sensual, inviting place by applying a warm colour palette or converted into a calm and relaxing haven by applying cool colours. Colour has the ability to translate the resonance of a visually stimulating moment and capture its essence.

A complex chameleon, colour is an enigma that adopts elements of its surroundings, as if by osmosis. Colour has its own dynamic and is affected by its environment – natural or artificial. Scale, lighting, surface finish, and saturation level all affect colour. Whether faded naturally or intentionally, sun-dried or textured, applied

Above Left A solitary red glass tumbler on a deep, stained-oak windowsill catches the natural daylight. It provides a moment of intense vibrant colour among the more subdued and sombre tones of the historical surroundings.

Left The deep buttoning of the Prussian blue velvet upholstery creates a secondary, almost geometric, motif, which gives the sofa a luxurious antique feel. The light catches the peaks of the surface, transforming them into a silver blue.

in translucent or opaque finishes, or in glossy or matt form, colour has a powerful resonance. It can dominate as a theme or simply appear as an accessory, emerging with all its changeable qualities as the major player in the creation of an interior. It can lead or follow, and in modern eclecticism very often confidently dances in and out of both roles. The modern eclectic approach defiantly encourages polychromatic anarchy, throwing colour wheels into the wind and preferring instead to rely on personal vision, inspiration, and imagination in the creation of an interior.

Below A blue-and-white-striped, cast glass dish sits on a contemporary white, satin-finished Formica table, which echoes the pattern within the dish and forms a visual connection with the other blue objects in the space.

Overleaf Left As sunlight reaches the fluid forms of Kate Hume's jewel-coloured glassware, an amber glow is cast over the surrounding floor area. By contrast, the floor is covered with a lino more often used in gymnasiums.

Overleaf Right The vivid, swirling effect of an aqua plastic-and-chrome kitchen chair adds a Mediterranean flavour, albeit with 1950s references, to the streamlined atmosphere of the steel and glass surroundings.

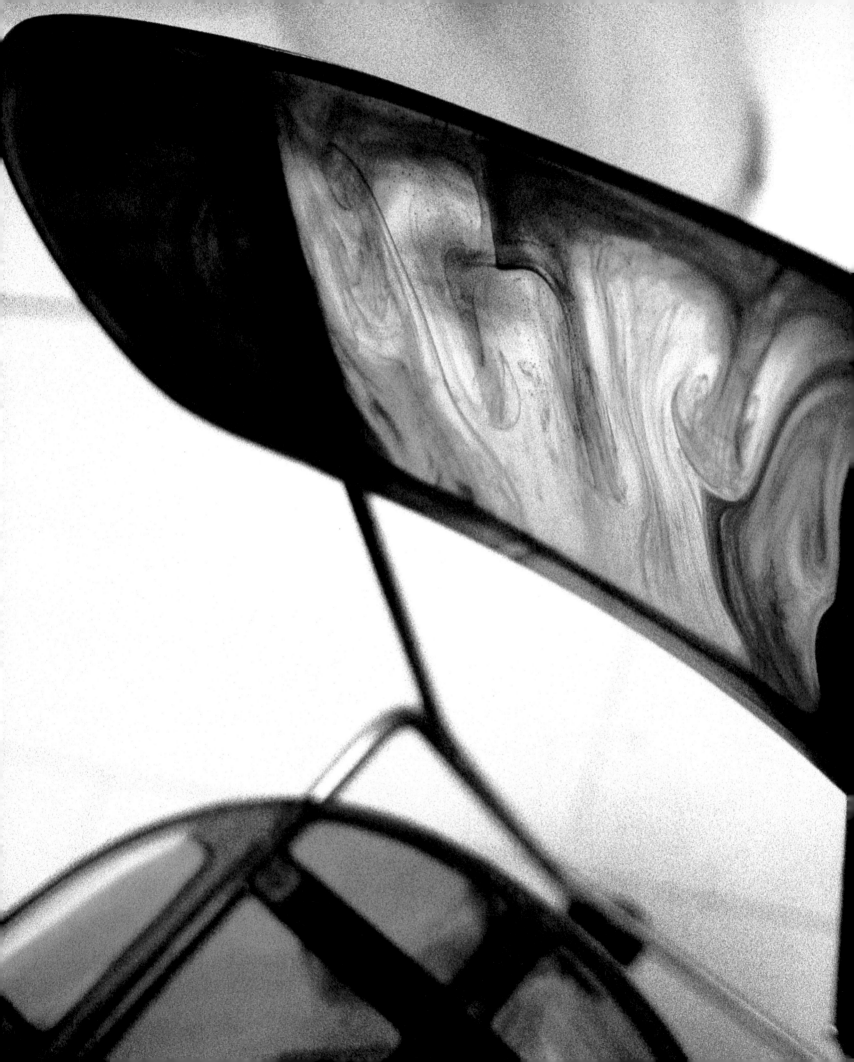

Above Left This electric blue lampshade was formed by hand-pleating fabric onto a frame and then finishing the bottom edge with a dramatic band of heavy blue-and-gold fringing. It was hand-made for a lamp base that was missing a shade.

Above Centre A hand-cut, long-stemmed, crystal wine glass, softly tinted rose, almost looks as if the wine has already been poured into it. The glass is part of a jewel-coloured collection, which provides a dramatic counterpoint to the glossy sheen of the polished wood dining table.

Above Right A grass green version of the now almost infamous plastic "dish doctor" washing-up rack by Marc Newson leans against the intricately patterned original tilework. The overall effect, like rows of green matchsticks, continues the circles and squares motif.

Below Left An 18th-century Italian gilded armchair, upholstered in red silk velvet damask and with ornately carved details, adds an air of baroque elegance to the dark oak-panelled Georgian library.

Below Centre A hand-blown Murano glass vase, bought in Venice, has been imaginatively turned into a lamp base by feeding the flex through a specially drilled hole under the lamp. When lit, the blue tones within the glass merge with those reflected into its surface, creating an organic self-pattern.

Below Right Originally found in a shop selling religious icons in Barcelona, this smoked glass naked lightbulb reveals a religious figure formed by the outline of the exposed orange filament.

Loft Apartment
Shoreditch
London

On the summit of a former factory building in Shoreditch, London, lies a large-scale urban retreat. Converted by designers' agent Naomi Cleaver and her partner Oliver, the loft provides the ultimate modern live/work environment. The apartment was purchased in shell form, consisting of a cavernous, concrete, 250sq m (2,688sq ft) space, lined by huge industrially proportioned windows on both sides. Attracted by the vast scale of the space and the architectural heritage of the building, Naomi and Oliver began exploring the extensive possibilities for conversion, letting the key architectural features inform their design decisions.

Central to their approach is the wall-hung antique fire door, now dominating the space in a purely decorative capacity. Its unique appearance – almost like a medieval castle door – lends the interior an air of urban romance and serves as a constant reminder of the industrial origins of the former factory. A mid-20th-century padded leather lounger and footstool sit in front of the metal door, acting as a transition from the historical to the contemporary and softening the overall effect. A steel spiral staircase rises from a square graphic bed of pebbles, inset into the polished wood-strip flooring, further highlighting the inherited industrial atmosphere of the original space.

The blend of the considered and the collected, the old and the new, continues in the living area. A white leather chair – a modern take on the traditional wing design – seems to emerge out of the matt white wall behind. Deep leather sofas, swathed in a collection of richly woven throws and surrounded by oversized sheepskin beanbags that invite lounging, give the area a relaxed, club-like ambience.

Because the basic shell of the apartment was constructed in concrete, installing recessed lighting without creating false walls and ceilings was not an option. Not wanting to lose the real framework of the space, Naomi and Oliver decided to turn this potential problem into a feature by using an eclectic collection of "one-off"

Right A strikingly bold three-colour palette of blue, crimson, and chalk white provides a perfect counterpoint to the antique oak bed and the top-hung door, which forms an asymmetrical headboard. The "Target" light by Totem draws the colours together.

free-standing lights, connected by coiled wires that hang across the space and bounce from socket to light source almost frivolously. Spanning a series of late 20th-century design movements, each light has its own identity, ranging from the quirkiness of the blue, pleated, glass-tasselled shade, perched on an organic Murano glass base, to the sleekness of the totemic long, red, glowing lightbox, mounted on the wall. Design classics accompany modern-day originals, each individually determining the atmosphere within their own light pool. Together this eclectic collection of lights perfectly expresses Naomi and Oliver's design philosophy of "making what we have work with where we want to go."

In order to divide the interior into living, working, and sleeping areas, without constructing internal walls that would permanently divide the space, Naomi and Oliver installed a series of modular wall units. This maintained the open-plan atmosphere of the apartment while offering the flexibility to reconfigure the space at a later date. A floor-to-ceiling unit at one end acts as a library for their extensive collection of books, while, at the same time, it creates a screened-off private bedroom area on the other side. The use

Above A Murano glass lamp sits on a "Target" table. The shade, made by Naomi, gives the lamp a boudoir-like quality. In contrast, the wall-mounted red Perspex light, originally a postcard dispenser by Spaced Out, provides a graphic block of neon.

of modular furniture systems has become more prevalent, particularly in open-plan interiors that double as live/work spaces. Flexible furniture systems offer the ability to transform a space from an area dedicated to a single function to a multifunctional space. Office areas within a domestic environment often are used predominantly during the day and can be transformed by screening off. Housing a desk area within a wall unit that can be retracted is another option and provides additional living space when not in use. This approach was adopted successfully by Naomi for the creation of her dedicated office area and maintains the open-plan atmosphere of the apartment while also offering the flexibility of reconfiguring the space at a later date. To create her own office area, Naomi commissioned British contemporary furniture designer Richard Dewhurst to design a unit that would marry form and function. The unit decorates the living area on one side with a series of backlit, primary-coloured, elongated Perspex squares, which on the other side fulfil all of Naomi's office storage requirements. This vibrantly coloured multifunctional piece also provides the dining area with an atmospheric focal point for night-time entertaining.

Above Right The blue, veneered, three-legged Formica "Polo" stool, a prototype by Jugganaut, provides a floating spot of colour among the expanse of stripped wood flooring. The colour connects with the matt blue wall at the opposite end of the space.

Right An antique, walnut, circular side table holds two vases – one, a white stemmed glass vase and the other a red Perspex vase. Together they form a three-dimensional version of the Constructivist framed print that leans on the wall behind.

Above The storage unit/room divider, with its inset panels of coloured Perspex, Formica, and wood, was custom-designed by Richard Dewhurst. The backlit panels on the dining room side provide a dramatic, vibrant backdrop for entertaining. The armchair establishes a visual link between the living and working areas.

For the dining area, Naomi wanted to create a versatile space that could accommodate large-scale entertaining, as well as a casual breakfast. Coming from a multi-skilled background that includes running her own catering company, Naomi designed an open-plan kitchen with a semi-professional feel. With its inherent industrial references, stainless steel seemed the natural choice of material. A length of stainless steel sheeting was used to line the rear wall behind the hob (stove) and sink, and form the work surface, complementing the exposed, surface-mounted, galvanized extraction pipes overhead. The kitchen cabinets were faced with wood to provide a link with the rest of the space. An overhead shelf runs the length of the kitchen and holds a collection of retro glass vases, large ceramic serving dishes, and a pile of well-thumbed cookery books. Below, a gaggle of shiny stainless steel cooking utensils hangs randomly. A long secondary breakfast bar, faced in padded leather and with a wooden work surface, separates the kitchen space from the dining area, creating an effect that is reminiscent of a 1960s airport lounge.

Colour plays a pivotal role in the design of the apartment, lending cohesion to a disparate collection of elements by providing continuity through different textures, forms, and surfaces. Colour has its own dynamic; it is affected by its immediate environment, by scale and saturation, by lighting, surfaces, and by the colour adjacent to it. Here a primary-colour palette was used to zone the space. Naomi uses colour in two different ways: solo, as a vibrant focal point to form a dominant signature, and as a unifying element to draw together architectural features and furnishings. In the first case, a bold, saturated, single block of colour is used on a wall or on a single piece of furniture, as in the Picasso blue wall that surrounds the windows and frames the exterior urban landscape, providing a link between the public and private area of the interior. Alternatively, colour is a vehicle for linking features, as in the soft honey tones that create a warm backdrop for the eating and food preparation area, which are punctuated by the vibrant egg-yolk yellow dining chairs placed around the slate-topped table.

The bedroom, known as the Blue Room, is furnished in a fusion of baronial and baroque styles. Rich velvet upholstery adorns the bed, which has a wall-hung, riveted, industrial door as a bedhead. Modern-designed lamps light a collection of inherited antiques, while a series of Persian rugs soften the floor area. Claret-toned walls lead the eye to an internal bathroom wall, lined with 1970s kingfisher-motif wallpaper. The bathroom is contemporary designed and split-level,

Below An antique Lloyd Loom chair sits between a minimal white floor lamp on a satin-finished chrome base and a micro version of the "Target" table, which holds a white long-necked vase. A claret-coloured wall picks up on the colours of the Persian rug.

with Far Eastern influences. Decking lines the floor and faces the bath, and a sandblasted shower screen with clear graphic circles separates washing functions from the bathing area. The effect is one of cool, textural calm set among the warm, saturated tones of the bedroom.

Ethnic elements make an ever-present statement within the apartment. The tall, floor-standing, ornately decorated striped pot and Aztec yellow woven throws in the living room recall South American holidays. The multicoloured, woven-plastic grocery curtain, masking the walk-in larder adjacent to the kitchen, almost seems to echo with the sounds of a local Middle Eastern souk. Surrounding the spiral staircase, which links the apartment with a private and equally vast roof terrace, is a vertical display of geometrically spaced, wall-mounted galvanized steel pots, filled with fuchsias and geraniums. Inspired by an exquisite Spanish courtyard that Naomi and Oliver had seen during their travels, the wall-mounted flowers form an organic transition from the interior to the sky-borne roof garden above.

A considered, vibrant, atmospheric apartment, filled with "one-off" design moments that are both inspiring and inviting, successfully fuses the inherited

with the designed, the monochrome with the technicolor. Although the interior was designed at the outset, the apartment has been allowed to evolve organically. Never ones to take themselves too seriously, albeit surrounded by a plethora of modern and retro design classics, Naomi and Oliver's wit permeates the space, as if by osmosis. Their lateral approach to a design challenge is perfectly illustrated by the television standing centre stage among the low-slung sofas, which are warmed by the glow from the screen, flickering with a virtual fire.

Above Positioned in front of the steel door is a 20th-century classic – an Eames armchair and footstool. Lit by a 1970s globe floor lamp on a chrome base by Guzzini, the area has a retro industrial feel. A recessed square of pebbles has a rug-like quality.

Left The honey-toned palette of the flooring is reflected in the yellow-upholstered dining chairs. The spiral staircase adds a "twist" to the geometry of the space, while the white leather armchair by Precious McBane provides a lightness of touch against a dramatic blue wall.

Apartment
Conversion
Amsterdam
Holland

Behind the Calvinistic façade of a former post office in Amsterdam's desirable antiques district, Kate Hume and Frans van der Heyden have created a vibrant, spacious, open-plan backdrop for their European lifestyle. Housing their collection of eclectic furniture, art, and accessories, the loft-like proportions of the apartment provide the perfect environment for living and showcasing their bold, dynamic, furniture and glassware ranges.

Originally based in New York, Kate and Frans, with respective careers in art direction and film commercials, decided to move back to Europe eight years ago. They chose Amsterdam as their European base and were originally looking for a *pied-à-terre* from which to live and run their Dutch film production company, Birdman Films, while also working on commissions in France and America. Having lived in an

enormous SoHo loft in New York, locating a space with equivalent proportions in Amsterdam was a challenge. Dutch houses, generally tall and narrow in proportion with steep ladder staircases, seemed small and restrictive. Finding the disused post office, with its industrial-size proportions, asymmetrical façade, and pitched roof was such a rarity that Frans put in an offer without seeing the interior, having only glimpsed the width and scale of the main staircase leading to the space.

Kate and Frans took an entire year to make the apartment habitable. It was what the Dutch call a *casco* – it had no electricity or heating – but provided them with a platform for their abundant creative talents. The fusion of their sophisticated design language with their collection of antique, contemporary, and own-designed pieces really expresses both Kate and Frans's design philosophy and their approach to the creation of their interior space. Taking a year to create the infrastructure of the apartment was a necessary process for them. As Frans says, "a good interior cannot be thrown together in a week."

The couple started with an empty shell – the original postmaster general's offices – clad in dark wood panelling. They

Right The living area is dominated by a large nude by Kees Maks. Giant pieces of Kate's glass stand on Frans's Birdman bench. A collection of 20th-century classics, such as the Marcel Breuer armchair and a wooden Rietveld chair, accompany the space.

removed internal walls to create a light, elemental, open, contemporary space, but retained key architectural features that gave the apartment its identity. With its high ceilings and huge windows, the apartment was flooded with natural light from both sides. The typically Dutch view to the front and views over rooftops to the back were reminiscent of New York.

The original dark wood architraving that divided the walls and lined all the door frames lent the space an overly retro atmosphere. So Frans, with his family background in architecture, designed a sleek, squared, modern architrave in oak to encase the original door frames and picture rails. Both design-led and practical, the oak cladding system also housed all the electric cabling, creating a streamlined framework for the apartment. The oak picture rail delineated the space and disguised the fact that the original panelling had made the walls uneven. It also provided the perfect place to display Kate's glassworks and the couple's extensive collection of art and photography. An open uncluttered space divided the living area from the kitchen. To retain the open-plan feel of the space, yet create a visual divide between the kitchen and the lounge, Frans designed a floor-to-

Above Left One of Kate's hand-blown organic fluid glass pieces, "t.figue," casts caramel-coloured shadows on the table below, while its amber interior holds a fish-eye reflection of the surroundings.

Below Left Bought 25 years ago in Hamburg, this leather-and-chrome chair, with its distressed leather seat shown in detail, is a Marcel Breuer classic. It sits on a burnt sienna kilim that is edged in a hand-finished blanket stitch.

ceiling glass-and-oak open partition with square panes. The partition reflected the Frank Lloyd Wright architectural references of the building and maximized the amount of light, particularly important in Amsterdam's darker winter months.

With the couple's finely tuned design sensibility and a refreshing ability to inject a touch of irony into the interior, the master bedroom is the only place where the original dark wood panelling has been left intact. In stark contrast to the light, lofty living area, the room has a resonance and depth that refer back to its former use as the postmaster general's office, yet also has a warmth that belies its official origins. The dark chocolate-truffle tones of the wood are highlighted by the honey-toned silk curtains, which frame the window. The original light oak map chest, inherited with the space, formerly had vertical drawers, but the piece was ingeniously converted by Frans to form a lateral chest of drawers. Above, a richly toned black-and-white Robert Doisneau photograph refers back to the dark wood panelling.

The bedrooms created for their two sons continue the light, minimal approach and are more functional, with each room featuring a floor-to-ceiling oak wall shelving unit in Frans's signature bold, graphic

style. The map drawers for the boys' rooms have been creatively adapted as under-bed storage units.

Even before launching the Birdman furniture range, Frans had always made furniture. As Kate says, "I used to say, 'We need a bed,' and he'd make one." Growing up within a family of architects and surrounded by wood materials, Frans developed an early interest in furniture,

Above A wenge version of Frans's Birdman "Board" holds Kate's almost liquid glass pieces and a vase by ceramist Barbara Jackson. Behind are three black-and-white photographs of Kate and their two sons, taken by Miep Jukkema. In front is an orange Charles Eames rocker. The electric guitar is an original Rickenbacker.

and started collecting chairs at the age of sixteen, a passion that continued even while pursuing his career as a photographer. His ability to extract the essential and reject the superfluous, a skill honed through his photography and later his art direction, manifests itself in the strident, graphic architectural forms of his furniture. Frans holds a fascination for "the timelessness that certain designs expose" and has a love of furniture "that has had a life before; vintage pieces that function well in conjunction with contemporary design." His furniture designs continue the

pared-down neutral ethos of the apartment's framework, which is punctuated perfectly by Kate's giant, almost liquid, fluid glass forms in semiprecious gem tones. At first, Kate created her bold, organic, hand-blown glass forms for her own pleasure and then used them as accessories to complement the smooth planes and angular lines of the Birdman furniture and lighting collection. However incidental their beginnings, Kate's glassware lines are now highly sought after. In fact, her entire collection has been bought by Donna Karan in New York, which now forms the basis of her internationally successful business.

The focal point of the living area is a large canvas of a nude, painted in an intense palette of hot colours by 1930s artist Kees Maks. Kate bought the painting twelve years ago and it has travelled with them, adorning the walls of their previous homes in New York and France. Kate admits that it is this painting that provided her with the colour scheme for the whole apartment. With her long-held passion for orange, Kate has brought the painting to life three-dimensionally through her choice of colours and textures in the interior. Using layers of hot chilli, burnt orange, and citrus shades, Kate mixes flat, saturated,

Below A series of original chairs by Eames, Hans Wegner, and Joe Atkinson for Michael Thonet, lean against the wall. Three of Kate's jewel-coloured vases, "Bottle," "Vessel," and "t.drop," cast long amethyst shadows on the gymnasium linoleum floor.

plain colours in felt and wool with richly patterned Middle Eastern throws bought in Morocco to create a warm, almost bohemian, atmosphere. Piles of vibrant single-coloured floor cushions, placed on top of one another in descending size, perch on the smooth satin-finished maple of one of Frans's elemental *chaise longues*. A vermilion rug, edged in yellow fringing, frames the wenge coffee table designed by Frans. A collection of Kate's glassware nestles on the pale oak Birdman bench. A variously sized fluid glass family, gloriously backlit, creates a theatre of colour in front of the windows in the living area. A lemon yellow, low-slung sofa, covered in wool bouclé by Dutch designer Martin Visser, acts as a visual divide between the living space and the lounge area. Key retro pieces by Gerrit Thomas Rietveld, Marcel Breuer, and Charles and Ray Eames, from Frans's extensive collection, form natural punctuation points to the polychromatic nucleus of the space.

The couple's extensive collection of photography and art confirms their eclectic taste. A huge photograph by Irving Penn, of two wine-filled glasses and a cigarette, hangs in the hallway. Kate says, "used to have it in the bedroom, but it made us feel as if we were sleeping in an ashtray."

Several of Frans's fashion shots hang next to beautifully framed, evocative, black-and-white portraits of Kate and the boys. Smaller paintings by Kees Maks rest on the oak dado rail. Opposite stands an antique display case filled with Kate's personal collection of *objets*, family photographs, some of her earlier glass pieces, and a series of Dutch ceramics. "My obsession with collecting these fantastic milky blue ceramics, popular in Holland in the 1930s, is well known among my friends. I suppose I am like any girl with a collection of things I just can't part with."

Above The original wood panelling in the bedroom was retained to give the space a sense of intimacy. On top of an original map chest, a series of Kate's glass forms are lit by one of Frans's Birdman lamps. A framed print by Robert Doisneau hangs above.

An effective and versatile way to introduce texture into an interior is to mix small, contrasting areas of texture on a furniture piece, over a wall finish, or on a large expanse of flooring. Textural zones can be subtly suggested by a shift from one material to another. For example, a smooth hardwood floor with a dramatic grain can be abutted to satin-finished stainless steel floor tiles, which in turn can move on to an area covered with a sumptuous hand-knotted silk rug.

As with colour, light affects the way a textural surface looks. As natural light falls upon a surface's uppermost layer, it is, in part, absorbed into the substrate, gradually changing the surface's outer appearance throughout the day. Light can be manipulated to bring about specific effects. By placing a dedicated artificial light source to the side of an object or surface, the finish can be highlighted. Placing a spotlight above a object will emphasize the outer layer, throwing inner recesses into deep shadow. By contrast, flooding a vertical plane with direct lighting will minimize any surface carvings, ornate detailing, or granulation.

Natural elements in the form of fresh flowers, plants, and exotic grasses introduce texture in its most elemental

Above Left An antique silk tassel hangs in front of shot-silk taffeta drapes. The drapes are minimally finished, simply wrapped over a plain wrought-iron pole, and the oversized tassel provides all the textural and decorative detailing necessary.

Below Left A collection of twigs has been fused together in this part art installation, part modular coffee table by artist Frank Morzuch. The five-piece work sits on 18th-century hexagonal tiles, which share the same references of charcoal and cream.

form, providing an organic layer that is imbued with a natural energy. Gathered together in graphic groups or arranged iconically to stand alone, these elements offer an accessible way to maintain our connection with the natural world, while affording the opportunity to express our creativity through a living art form.

Modern eclecticism takes textural surfaces and finishes out of their natural habitat and drops them into a new context, where they are juxtaposed with complementary and contrasting elements. An interior is the perfect arena within which

to explore the infinite creative possibilities that the application of texture can provide. From the smallest textural accessory to the broad sweeps of a bamboo-lined wall, texture adds dimension to an interior. The exploration of all surfaces, whether man-made or natural, manufactured or recycled, is fundamental to the modern eclectic approach. With an unending repertoire of players in the theatre of texture, the modern eclectic approach replaces the expected with the surprising, and in doing so creates an interior that can be as enigmatic as it is experimental.

Above Exposed brickwork has been painted white to create a neutral canvas, yet retain textural emphasis, and random applications of gold leaf add interest. Windows are half covered by a contemporary treatment of woven graphite fabric.

Overleaf Left This detail of a table lamp by designer Georgia Scott reveals an intricate yet geometric design formed out of steel wire mesh. When lit, a woven spangled light pattern is cast on the immediate surroundings.

Overleaf Right This antique metal folding chair, which pivots shut, was originally designed for use as a garden chair. Although roughly finished, it has a surprising elegance that is emphasized by the secondary motif on the seat and its fluid lines.

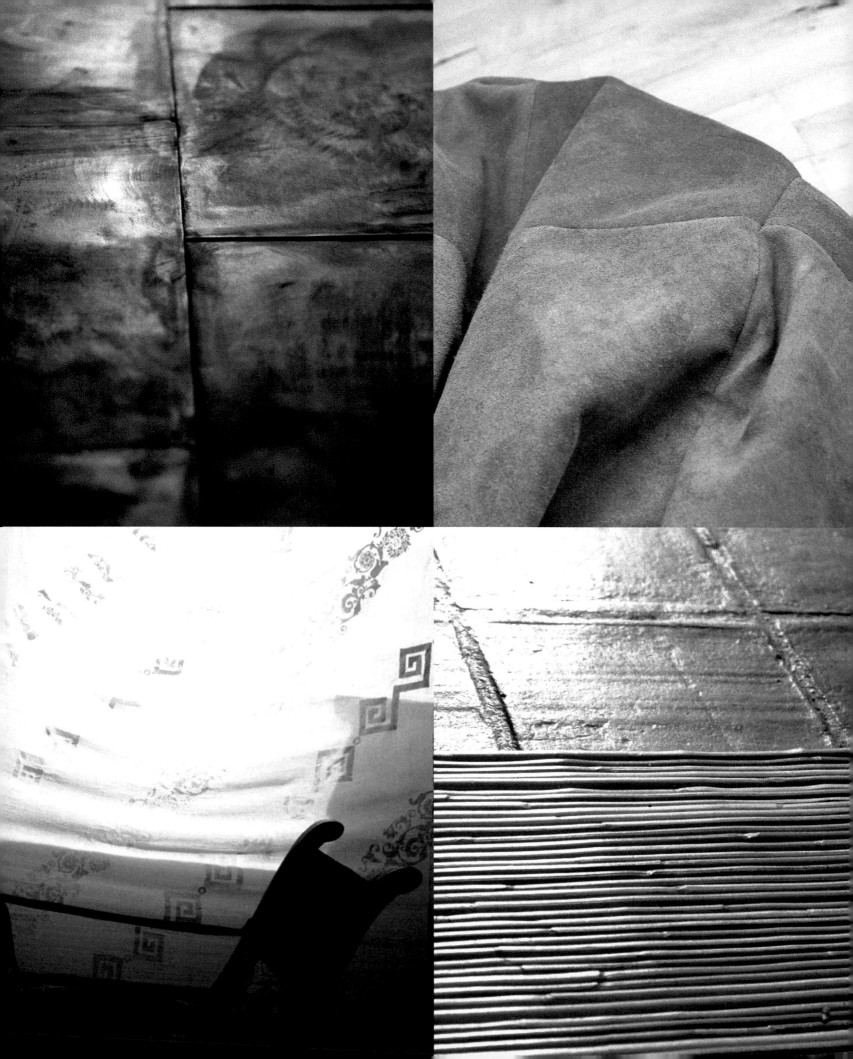

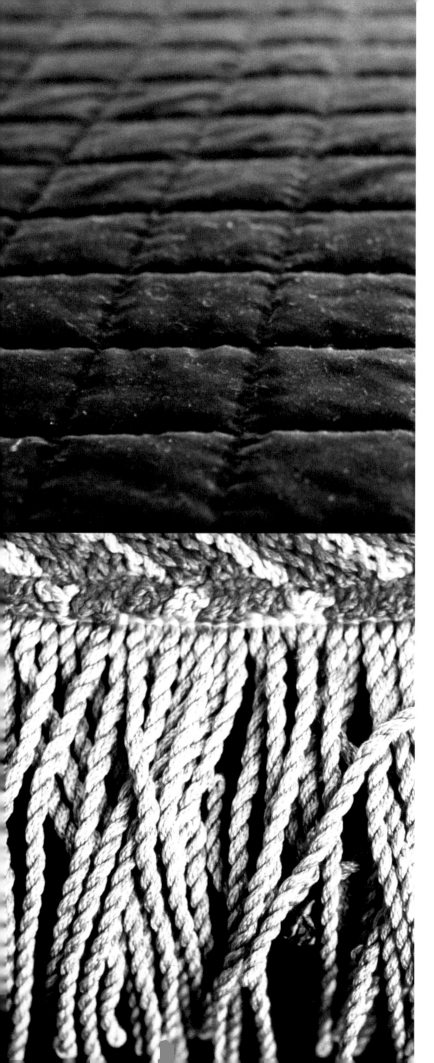

Above Left The patina of the dark slate floor tiles, which line the kitchen area, refer back to the slate worktop on the breakfast bar, above, and to the dining table on the other side of the space. The riven texture of the tiles adds visual interest to the floor while providing a practical nonslip surface.

Above Centre An oversized toast-coloured suede beanbag provides an organic resting point among the sweep of pale blonde wood-strip flooring.

Above Right A simple padded velvet throw in deep mahogany provides a sensual, tactile element to the space. The throw retains a contemporary feel through its geometric lines of stitching.

Below Left A white hand-embroidered Parisian sheet is threaded onto two vertical metal poles like a banner, providing an elemental window dressing. The curtain is opaque enough to provide privacy, but translucent enough to flood the room with diffused natural light.

Below Centre The hand-baked, locally crafted terracotta tiles form the perfect floor-level background to a tatami mat. The junction between the two textures provides a seamless transition from the quadratic to the linear.

Below Right The extra-long, twisted fringing framing this antique tapestry cushion adds medieval splendour to the piece and lends a sense of theatre to the leather chair on which it is placed.

18th-century Manor House Luberon France

Tucked away on the outer slopes of a tiny medieval village, in the hills of the Luberon, between Arles and Avignon in France, stands an 18th-century manor house. Inside, Kamilia Regent and Pierre Jaccaud are living the life most people would classify as a "dream."

Pierre, a set designer, and Kamilia, an art dealer with her own gallery, were previously caught up in the "urban chaos," as Kamilia describes it, of professional life in Brussels. In 1993, yearning to "get a life and re-start living surrounded by sunshine and distant hills," they decided that they were ready to make the break and leave the city. Filled with thoughts of Tuscan hillsides and Italian cobbled streets, no one was more surprised than they when the couple fell in love with Saignon, the 18th-century stone manor house that is now their home, during a holiday in South-East France.

The house is steeped in a history that spans centuries, and had been immaculately preserved. For Pierre and Kamilia, it was a dream realized. Originally the property belonged to an established Swiss family, who had founded the Red Cross and who had bought the house at the turn of the last century with the proceeds from selling an original manuscript by Goethe. With its grandeur of scale, thick stone walls, richly patterned 18th-century tilework, and frondescent grounds filled with fruit trees overlooking the wild, almost austere, countryside of the Luberon, the house was imbued with a rich cultural heritage. It offered Kamilia and Pierre a textural and spatial haven within which to establish their home, "living" art gallery, and artists' residence.

The house was bought with all the furniture and contents, which provided the couple with the perfect platform to "edit, add, and subtract." Working with, and around, the inherent textural and architectural features was both a joy and a challenge. Pierre's set design background enabled him to address the structural alterations to the house. These "enhancements," as he calls them, were undertaken with a subtlety and sensitivity to the integrity of the house, so that they

Right The hallway beyond the 18th-century riveted wooden front door is rendered in a plaster-and-cement finish. A series of muslin panels suspended from equidistantly spaced tension wires, created by artist Veit Stratman, is lit by a black metal lamp.

blend almost seamlessly with the original. Some of the smaller spaces were opened out, vertically and laterally, through the formation of narrow slits, cut out from the 2m (6 $\frac{1}{2}$ft) thick walls. Glass panels were inserted into walls like works of art, creating tantalizing vignettes by allowing a glimpse into another section of the house. Cobbled walls relinquished central sections to create rough-hewn archways.

With her background in art, Kamilia undertook the internal decoration with the same vision that she would have previously bestowed on an exhibition of installations. With an 800sq m (8600sq ft) arena spread over three floors within which to work, she began to undertake the sensual, multilayered harmonizing of ancient and modern, texture and tone, patterned and plain. Taking direction from each space and almost letting the key features lead her, Kamilia worked organically, rather than imposing a design scheme onto the space. Inspired by the southern golden light that turned the countryside into a vibrant, florid canvas, she ascribed to each room a dominant chalk-based hue from the natural palette that surrounded her.

Employing the richly saturated colour and texture of chalk-based paint on the

Above Left The patina of age has transformed this antique table from a simple mahogany country table into a three-dimensional textural masterpiece. The table's cracked and pitted surface has been proudly left on show.

Below Left On the buttercup yellow wall, facing the French doors that lead to the garden, Kamilia has wall-mounted numerous test tubes, filled with ink-coloured water. Each tube contains a stalk of budding carnation.

smoother internal walls and a tinted plaster finish for some of the rougher walls, Kamilia used local colours and finishes throughout the interior. Original wooden doors and window frames were left unaltered, providing a textural framework to each room. The floors, covered in original 18th-century tiles, were perfectly preserved, so they were simply re-polished to provide a series of patterned surfaces – a perfect counterpoint to the simple saturated colour of the walls. Windows were softened with lengths of sorbet-coloured silk taffeta panels, lined in hot acid colours, and hung on locally made wrought-iron poles. After setting the scene for each room, Kamilia initially proceeded to select key works from her extensive art collection to act as a visual anchor for each space. Every area within the house was designed to have its own unique identity, but at the same time to establish a connectivity between the spaces through an undercurrent of blended organic textures and materials.

Pushing open the huge, heavy, riveted exterior door reveals a long narrow hallway. On one side, the corridor is faced with an undulating, roughly plastered, ecru wall; on the opposite side, a series of long, gently billowing, almost diaphanous,

bleached muslin panels hang effortlessly and equidistantly behind each other. This installation, one of an annual series produced by artist Veit Stratman, sets the scene for the creative voyage of discovery to follow within the interior.

The lounge, designed around a motif based on the geometric charcoal-and-cream floor tiles, has a calm, gentle elegance. At first glance, the room seems imbued with a surprising sobriety. It is decorated in a palette of muted hues, from the midnight blues that cover the furniture to the subtle tonal abstract paintings that

Below The lounge area features huge grey monochromatic paintings by New Zealand artist Nicolas Reese. A delicate twig installation by Frank Morzuch hangs in front of the glass internal window, leading the eye to the gallery area next door.

Above On either side of the balcony doors in one of the studio suites stand two 19th-century totem poles of horses, originally used in house construction. A diverse collection of chairs, including antique gilded "Opera" chairs and a one-off "Dalí" chair by a local artist, surround a marble-topped table. A splash of yellow is provided by Wlodzimierz Pawlak's painting, entitled *Homage to Van Gogh*.

line the walls. However, in exploring the space further, Kamilia's presence is ever-felt in the neon-lit installation of plastic bottles by Bill Cuthbert, wall-mounted above the dark glossy piano. In the centre of the floor, a series of logs are fused vertically together to form an organic modular coffee table. At one end of the room, in front of a glass panel cut into the wall, hangs an exquisite installation of rows of horizontal twigs, created by artist Frank Morzuch. The facing wall exhibits a giant contemporary fireplace, filled with logs, and takes the organic motif of a

floating forest and seems to convert the abstract into the actual with a crackling, roaring fire.

The dining room is dominated by a long, antique wooden table and two simple wooden benches, with the patina of the wood worn and crackled by the years. Every evening the table is brought to life with a communal supper prepared by Kamilia, feeding the friends, resident artists, and visitors staying at the house. The walls, colourwashed in *eau de Nil*, frame a dramatic 18th-century black marble fireplace. Two wall-mounted naked light bulbs with orange filaments illuminate portraits of Kamilia and Pierre. The paintings, vibrantly contemporary, maintain the owners' presence even when they are absent.

The first floor houses three of the six bedrooms, each painted a different vivid colour and filled with a collection of antiques, original art, and installations. Within each one, the perfect blend of nature and culture is achieved, interspersed with inevitable moments of wit – illustrated perfectly by the oversized plaster fish key-rings allocated to each room. The rooms, each introduced by a different antique door, are connected by a long internal hallway lined with roughly

Right Studio space has been left as a raw canvas for artists. Sally Ross's monochrome of Peter Sellers has an eerie lifelike quality, which connects with the "Orb" painting, left. The photo-art cubes are by Voly Fangor.

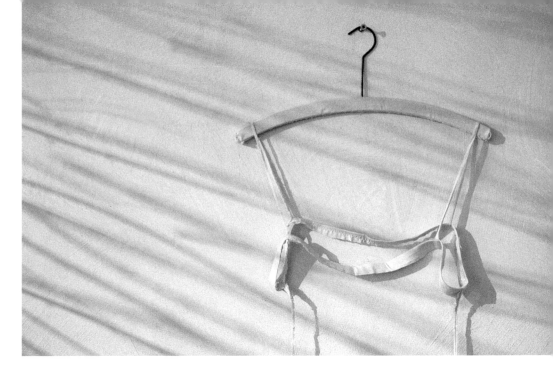

rendered walls, which provide the perfect counterpoint to the satin sheen of the geometric 18th-century floor tiles. All rooms have views onto the garden outside – a lush, verdant tableau of fecund trees, heavy with fruit, and punctuated with a series of huge bronze felinesque sculptures, resting in the long grass.

The three loft studios on the second floor have endlessly high ceilings and a combination of roughly cemented and stone walls. Refreshingly raw, with unvarnished, rough wooden floors, these cavernous spaces are interrupted by exposed galvanized steel pipes. The scale of space serves as a reminder of the building's history and its new incarnation as a retreat for visiting artists. Operating on the principle established by the Impressionists – the exchange of art for accommodation – Kamilia and Pierre have opened the house for artists to come and stay, the only condition being that they leave a piece of work when they leave. The effect this has on the interior means that the house is always evolving. As new artworks are left by artists, the balance of the space shifts and is reworked once again. For Kamilia and Pierre, "the house is a continuing celebration of the creative process," which has brought them several

steps closer to fulfilling their joint ambition of "bringing contemporary art to life."

Almost like living in the ultimate rotating stage set, Saignon attracts an international following of artists, writers, and visitors fascinated to partake in the unique experience that this almost Medici villa provides. It seems almost implausible, when surrounded by the exquisite, textural artscape within this manor house, to ask Kamilia and Pierre if they miss anything about their previous urban life. As Pierre says, "Paris is no further than the end of our garden – we have distanced ourselves from the world so that it can come and join us here." For the couple, the space that they have created is more than a home; it operates on many levels over and above the purely aesthetic. "For us it is art that informs every pore of our being and the way that we live," Pierre says. "The house writes its own history. It is an improvisation – people come and find their place."

Above An installation by Pip Cuthbert adorns a lounge wall. This simple yet powerful piece lets the eye and the imagination fill in the spaces. Her work – so feminine, so ephemeral – has a long-lasting resonance and refers to the twig installation next to it through the delicacy and soft-hued subtlety they both share.

Left In Saignon, even a hallway has become a living gallery. The neon-lit chair is by Bill Cuthbert. An installation by Pip Cuthbert uses woven strands on hangers to echo past and future forms, and the door is an artwork by Koen Theys.

Town House
Catalunya
Spain

Standing on the edge of the central square in the Catalan town of Pallfrugell in northern Spain is a building with Art Nouveau inspired details. Formerly a bank, it is now home to Izabella Leszczynska and Patrice Carlhian, and their contemporary art and furniture gallery. Izabella, an artist and designer, and Patrice, a contemporary art dealer with a successful gallery in Paris, decided to make this town in Catalunya their permanent home four years ago. The quality of life they had experienced there during numerous holidays was eventually too hard to leave.

The flat-fronted three-storey building, with its elegant proportions and architectural detailing, shines like a beacon of modernism among the cobbled streets of its medieval surroundings. Drawn by the grandeur of the space and the volume of the house, Izabella and Patrice were instantly filled with ideas for creating a combined gallery and home. Inspired by the history of the building and its unexplored potential, they decided to buy the property in order to establish a permanent base in, as Izabella describes it, "this country of light."

The house is a rare example of architect Pellaio Martinez's work. Constructed in 1932, the original façade had been covered in local hand-crafted ceramics and an Art Nouveau glass-and-wrought-ironwork canopy hung over the main entrance. However, when the house was taken over for use as a bank, many of the original features were stripped out to create an environment more suitable for its commercial applications. Suspended ceilings were installed to house contract lighting, and large-scale rooms were partitioned to create offices. With the architect's original plans in hand, Izabella and Patrice began restoring the building to its former state. They also used the opportunity to implement some structural changes that would maximize the ground floor space they had allocated for the gallery, as well as the living areas above.

A grand sweeping staircase dominates the ground floor and links the gallery space to the living quarters. Lined with an

Right One of Izabella's art pieces lights the sweeping marble staircase. The large-format abstract was painted by Izabella by the sea. Below sit a collection of glassware by Silla and some of Izabella's plaster-and-ceramic forms.

intricate wrought-iron balustrade and hand-turned wooden banister, this original marble staircase provides a dramatic focal point. Originally designed to be on the opposite side of the building, Patrice and Izabella decided to restore the staircase but leave it where it was – appreciating the historical reference and sense of local context that it lent their newly formed contemporary environment. In order to open out the space to create a large gallery area, arches were cut out of all the dividing walls. The floor, although originally tiled, had been mostly destroyed through years of wear and tear. Rather than cover all traces of the tilework, areas that could be restored were incorporated into a new pressed granite floor, thus creating a visual link between the building's past and its future. The original walls were "sweating," due to the humidity of the local climate. Rather than scraping them back and dry lining them, Izabella decided to turn this potential problem into an inspiration for "a moving, evolving work." She covered the walls in red-tinted polyurethane varnish and then painted a series of textural tableaus onto them. As the walls continue to "sweat," the paint changes colour and moves, recreating the art works into modified versions of the originals.

Above Left The locally crafted table lamp on a wrought-iron stand was a find in Izabella's local flea market. The African tapestry underneath softens the effect, adding texture to the dark wooden antique desk.

Below Left A metal sculpture holds an aquiline porcelain dish; together the pieces create a new artwork. Izabella's abstract painting hanging above, *Summer Fields of Golden Flowers*, is another of her acclaimed "Earth" series.

At the back of the space, huge windows and a set of French doors reveal a "raw sculpture garden," filled with a disparate collection of chairs and seats, seemingly disenfranchised from their origins. A collection of Izabella's works in various stages of completion is dotted around – some almost seeming to grow into their surroundings.

The fusion of the organic elements of the surroundings with local colours and materials inspires and informs Izabella's work. She adopts the same expansive vision in her art and sculpture as in her

Above Hanging above the sofa in the lounge is a three-dimensional work by Luis Tomasello, lit by a vellum light. A 12th-century bust from Indonesia is mirrored on the other side of the sofa by a sculptural work entitled "Homage to Miró" by Catalan artist Viñas.

interior design. These original works form and fill the gallery, lacing the space with a textural three-dimensional inscription.

In true Catalan tradition, her work responds to the changing seasons. For the international annual flower show in Girona she was commissioned to produce a piece of artwork inspired by flowers.

Izabella chose to design and produce a piece using real red rose petals, but found that they would wilt during the course of the show, so she substituted silk petals. The petals cover a sheet of Perspex, with a concealed light source behind creating a translucent and delicately lit artwork on a metal stand. The piece is now back in their gallery, wall-mounted to light the staircase.

The gallery explores the connections between the contrasting elements of the works contained within it. Black wrought-iron forms, almost tribal and naïve in ethos, hold perfectly polished, sleek glass forms. Dramatic textural canvases translate local landscapes into planes of abstract colour and provide muted backdrops for contemporary Italian leather furniture. Local tiles are constructed into sun-baked, coloured, glossy cubes and mounted on top of each other to form geometric totem poles. Giant painted concrete platters hold a series of clear glass orbs. The hand-turned sit beside the hand-carved; the painted are next to the patinated; and the exotic translate into the etched.

Following the staircase to the first floor, the landing is framed on either side by two arches, each filled with the original leaded-glass doors. On one side a continuation of the gallery space is revealed; on the other side is the living area, kitchen, and terrace. Indicative of the Catalan way of "living outside," the living area seems to be an inverted extension of the terrace. Low-slung individual seating lines the stone balustrade, which in turn overlooks the palm trees in the garden below, giving the space an almost Moorish atmosphere. Inside original abstract art in neutral textures fills the walls. A huge vellum wall-mounted light continues the warm tones of sunlight after dark. A powerful sculpture made of oxidized iron provides a dramatic counterpoint to the white contemporary sofa and wall behind it. Locally produced original tiles create a graphic, almost grid-like effect of diagonals on the floors.

An open stone staircase runs up the wall parallel to the kitchen area, leading to the second floor, which contains the sleeping and bathing areas. Each of the three bedrooms was designed individually and feature a collection of unique antiques, artworks, and contemporary glass pieces. Opening one of the original hand-carved dark wooden doors reveals a hand-embroidered length of fabric hanging in front of the window, diffusing the sunlight. An ornate antique wooden table from a convent, used as a desk, stands in

silhouette in the light. A folding wood-and-leather chair, softened by a feather-filled cushion, accompanies the table. The butter-coloured walls are covered in a patinated plaster-and-cement finish, which complements the honey-hued hand-baked glazed terracotta tiles on the floor, and a heavy woven white throw turns

Below Stretched across the wall of the exhibition space is a diptych by Izabella, which resonates with depth and colour and establishes the palette for the room. In front stands another of her flower-inspired series of lit artworks. Standing on the diagonally laid tiles is an antique Indian teak table.

Left The bathroom is a contemporary haven with Zen references, formed mostly out of concrete on-site. The walls have a tinted cement render, which complements the raised walnut floor. A rattan blind masks the bathroom from the adjoining bedroom.

the bed into a textural centrepiece. By contrast, the bathroom is entirely contemporary. Concrete forms the space, with circular portholes opening views in the walls. A raised walnut wooden floor becomes a platform to contain the bath, giving it a sunken Eastern quality. Burnt sienna plaster-and-cement walls refer back to the Catalan context, while an open doorway, masked by a rattan screen, provides a glimpse of the bedroom.

Through their unique creative vision and talent, Izabella and Patrice have been pivotal in taking their genre of art and

design to an international audience. In the process, they have created a completely unique home from a series of contrasting yet cohesive textural compositions.

While their gallery has become a nucleus for local residents and visitors that share their contemporary aesthetic, their home has become the unofficial epicentre for nocturnal socializing. Once the gallery doors have shut, selected guests ascend the marble staircase to the terrace, where a contemporary renaissance of the "salon" thrives to the sound of classical music, crickets, and conversation.

Below The antique leather folding chair, "a general's chair used in Napoleonic times by the army," looks pastoral in this setting and faces the table, originally from a local convent. The large painting by Henry Closon on the left continues the buttermilk tones of the walls.

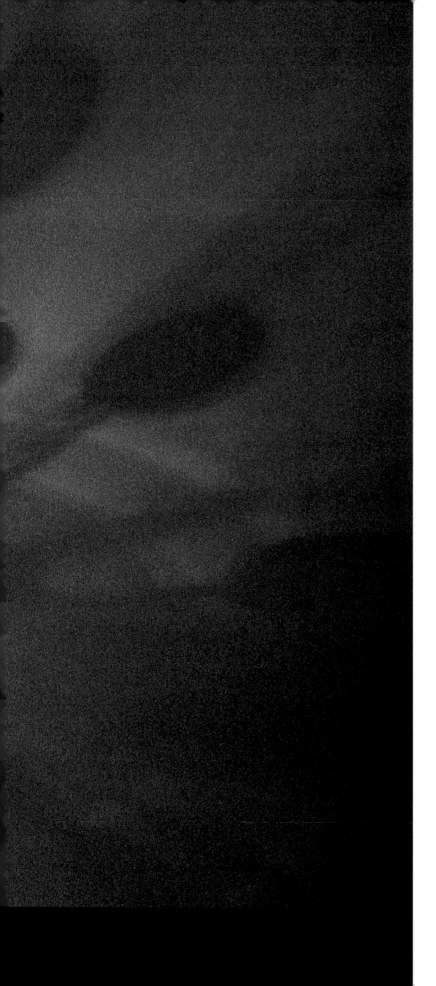

Pattern

Pattern is complex by nature; it is filled with a plethora of visual information that evokes responses. Our relationship to pattern is interactive and, like relationships, can hold an emotional dimension. A particular pattern can have a resonance that is as strong as a piece of music or particular fragrance. It can trigger memories or a sense of *déjà vu*, holding a key to a past experience by recalling a particular person, place, or atmosphere previously experienced. Loaded with references, sometimes overt but more often subliminal, pattern can, in a modern eclectic environment, introduce a sense of history and cultural heritage that can be either personal or chronological, albeit re-invented in contemporary form.

In modern eclecticism pattern is an overt antithesis to minimalism, and its applications can be as kaleidoscopic as its permutations. Traditional patterns hold a suggestion of a bygone era, of another time and place, acting as a reminder of the lives of previous generations and of the atmosphere of that period. However, the approach to pattern is more reductionist in modern eclecticism. Pattern is often initially introduced into an interior purely as a graphic motif, with its inherent references and characteristics establishing atmosphere and context as a secondary role. Key patterns can be used to create a background, dominate the foreground, or can be layered to blur the edges between the two. In modern eclecticism "out of context," whether by design or default, is the manifestation of abstracted and reworked design preconceptions.

Pattern can be introduced into an interior in varying degrees. By turning up the volume to the "max" – for example, by using flourishing motifs and repeated geometry, pattern can stimulate. A pattern can be layered by piling an exaggeration of a pattern over a statement of it, over merely a suggestion. A single motif, repeated in clashing colours, can provoke a strong response; a pattern repeated through different substrates and interpretations can make a dramatic statement. On the other hand, low-volume "whispering" self-patterns offer motifs that are created through texture, such as in brocades and damasks which often have a three-dimensional quality and energy that surface-printed fabrics lack.

Decorative patterns can be inspired by paintings. Gustav Klimt created sumptuous, multicoloured tableaus; Van Gogh painted fields of colour; Matisse's work has an iconic graphic fluidity; and

Above Left The fine, almost skeletal, lines of an aluminium sculpture curve from a central "spine" like a giant fishbone and juxtapose with soft-edged, hand-painted squares applied directly onto the pigmented plaster wall.

Above Right The handcrafted mosaic table introduces both pattern and a Mediterranean atmosphere to the kitchen. The stone-tiled floor and stainless steel units around the table, although neutral, are washed with an aquatint from the mosaics.

Below Left Antique textiles are used as wall coverings, layered over each other to leave tantalizing edges on view. In front, a carved picture frame is filled with opaque glass, behind which a hand-applied circular motif emerges in almost shadow form.

Below Right The intricate patterns carved into this antique Balinese tabletop have a textural quality and depth that have become more accentuated with age. Grooved areas have become deeper toned, while raised areas have become worn and faded.

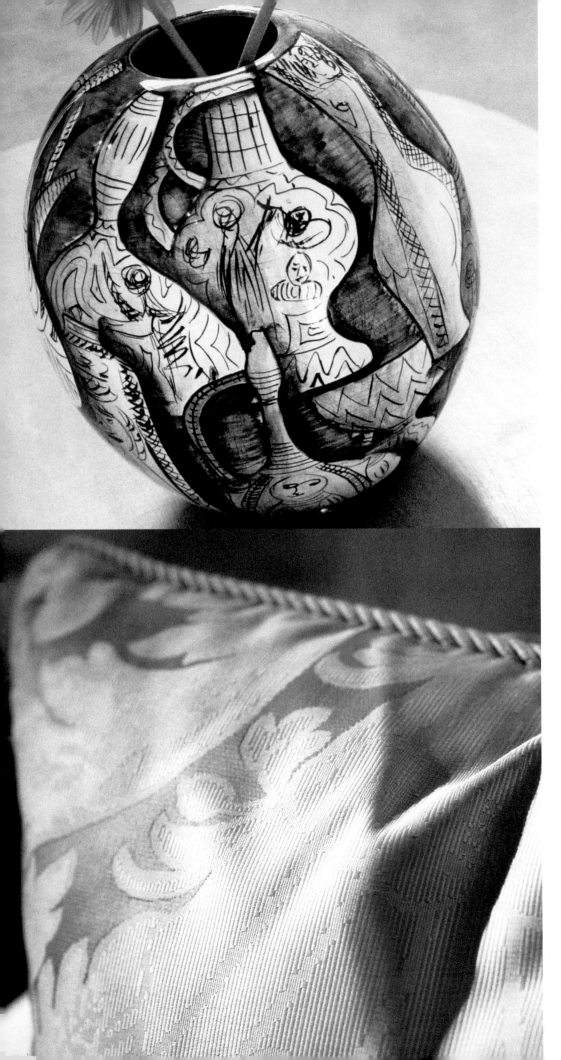

Seurat explored the possibilities of dots with his pointillist style. The sublime geometry of Mondrian's colour blocks has inspired a plethora of works. The architect Antonio Gaudí elevated the use of three-dimensional pattern to a new art form with the creation of the Sagrada Familia cathedral in Barcelona, crowned by spiralling patterned towers, which give the impression of being covered in layers of giant polychromatic mosaics. The work of Gaudí spawned an entire movement, and his influence is still visible in the use of mosaic in contemporary urban interiors.

Pattern can be applied directly onto surfaces by painting or gilding. It can be re-introduced in three-dimensional form as cornicings or highlighted in contrasting tones to pick out architectural detail. In woven form, pattern also adds texture, which can be introduced into an interior as accessories. On flooring, the inherent pattern of the substrate can be worked further by the laying arrangement, as in parquetry or tiling effects. Embossed, printed, photographic, and woven wall coverings can be juxtaposed, exploring the relationship between each one.

Introducing nature's organic patterning into an interior adds pattern in a more elemental way. Set against a constructed

Above Left The hand-painted monochromatic vase, although figurative, has a graphic, etch-like quality that is reminiscent of the work of Escher. It brings an area of dramatic pattern to the smooth marble table upon which it is placed.

Below Left A silk-and-linen damask, incorporating the natural tones of sand and driftwood, creates a secondary self-pattern within this decorative cushion cover. The linear texture of the warp threads provides a counterpoint to the sweeping floral motifs.

background, "living" forms such as plants and flowers inject a natural pattern, colour, and texture into an interior. Nature itself continues to be a source of inspiration; wild flowers and fruits, tropical fish, peacocks, and so on, all provide a rich visual vocabulary to fire the imagination.

The pattern of clutter, whether inadvertent or controlled, can have as much visual impact as more formal design elements. Representing a welcome informality and randomness, areas that are more chaotic and less ordered provide a touch of irreverence to a contemporary interior. Coloured glasses throwing patterns of dappled light onto surfaces or a collection of postcards creating a repeat pattern on a wall can create a secondary three-dimensional layer of pattern, while making a uniquely personal statement.

The anarchic relationship of pattern to modern eclecticism can be likened to that of Punk to contemporary music: it plays a major role in driving a medium into a new direction by deconstructing established key elements, which, when reassembled, form a pioneering new genre. More abstract than representational, more analogous than obvious, the use of pattern is imbued with an unself-conscious desire to explore the "shock of the new."

Above This chrome cuboid mini table, decorated with concentric circles and squares, is typical of the 1960s. It perfectly encapsulates the design ethos of that period and refers to the shapes Verner Panton and Victor Vasarely explored in their works.

Overleaf Left The almost tribal patterning of this ceramic vase, created by South African ceramist Barbara Jackson, fuses the cultural with the contemporay. The vase seems to be imbued with an inherent fragility despite its strident patterning.

Overleaf Right The glass shade of the table lamp, c.1970, fuses organic and asymmetrical forms, and seems to visually capture the essence of its era. Only the patterned central section is lit, highlighting the three-dimensional aspect of the lamp.

Above Left The intricate, undulating surface pattern created by the mother-of-pearl inlay on this antique Persian cabinet works in harmony with the curves of the drawers and the heavy white marble top. The drawer handles are made of hand-painted porcelain and finished with brass fixings.

Above Centre An original "one-off" textile, used as a wall hanging, has been made by layering small embroidered squares onto a metallic background. A striped fabric forms the central focal point.

Above Right A detail of Alessandro Mendini's "Proust" armchair reveals an almost pointillistic approach, albeit with tiny squares instead of dots. Interestingly, the pattern of the upholstery continues seamlessly onto the ornate carved wood frame that surrounds the chair back.

Below Left A corner of this 17th-century embroidered sampler, used as a table runner, reveals the original velvet fabric as almost without pile. The tones emerging through the velvet complement the embroidery and give an air of frayed fragility.

Below Centre An antique Japanese kimono, covered with both a printed and embroidered pattern, hangs against a dark oak wall panel like a textile. A work of art in its own right, it is still used by its owner.

Below Right The elaborate wood frame of this elegant 18th-century chair has been gilded to highlight the carving and refers back to the variegated motif on the silk velvet upholstery.

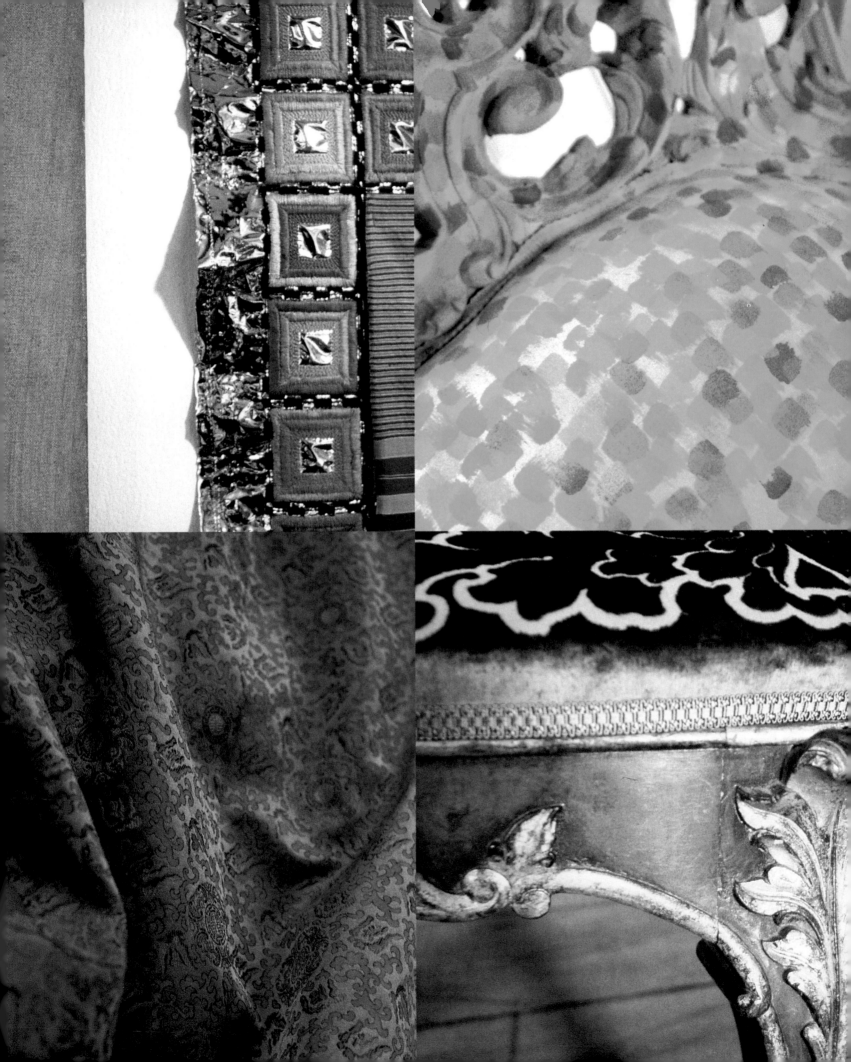

Apartment
New York
USA

Hidden within a monolithic apartment block in the heart of New York lies an intoxicating example of interior design, so personal that it defies categorization. Like a controlled polychromatic explosion, every inch has been decorated using the unique blend of intelligence, inspiration, and irony that belongs to its owner, Joe Holzman.

Design has featured strongly in Joe's life since childhood. Growing up with the three B's – beige, bland, and Baltimore, he developed a craving for pattern and colour. Joe spent his formative years surrounded by the neutral monotonal palette and recessed architectural lighting of his parents' home. Objects that would generally be taken for granted held an intense fascination for him, "a table lamp was an exotic object – lamp light thrilling," and he goes on to admit that his considered fest of patterned eclecticism is born of an inherent rebelliousness against all things measured and moderate.

As editor-in-chief and artistic director of cult interior design publication *Nest*, Joe is surrounded by design. His exploration of design ideology flows seamlessly from the walls of his apartment to the pages of his magazine – its title appropriately describing the creative process he adopts in both mediums. His interior is created in the same way as a nest, by assembling a plethora of collected pieces, which fuse together and bond to form a home. No surface, wall, door, or ceiling has been left unadorned. Ceiling joists are delineated with bold, geometric, black bands, outlining the architectural infrastructure of the space. Above the windows, a shelf holds a collection of several hundred art and design catalogues, their spines lined up perfectly to form a floating "barcode" at ceiling level. Even the humble venetian blind has metamorphosed into a hand-painted geometric tableau. Radiators are boxed in using a Braille-like motif of punched holes on the covering. Layer upon layer of objects, art, and furniture – from the minuscule Knoll sofa prototype to the majestic ornately gilded console – nestle on layers of rugs, textiles, and even the occasional plastic picnic cloth.

Right The lounge area is delineated at ceiling level by thick, bold, black stripes, making the supporting beams almost disappear. Immediately below, hundreds of art catalogues are lined up on a shelf, a testament to Joe's passion for art.

Nothing is quite what it seems here. The obvious is only a starting point on a journey through a series of layers to the obscure, the usual being replaced by the unique on the way. Even the seemingly white walls are, as Joe is quick to point out, "not white at all, but made up of three different tones of the lightest blues – all applied by hand in pointillistic dot form." The walls introduce a micro version of the circular motif that recurs in a variety of manifestations throughout the interior.

Starting with what Joe describes as "a disappointing shoebox rental apartment," the major limitation was not being able to make any structural changes. Working within the existing infrastructure, Joe started to define the space by creating a series of three-dimensional surfaces throughout the apartment by layering painted pattern, textile, *objets trouvés*, and art. Working outside the normal parameters of space or scale, he installed a full-sized grand piano in the lounge and used original artworks as "wallpaper – to cover a wall surface." Antique hand-woven silk rugs provide a wall-mounted decorative backdrop to contemporary abstract art pieces. Numerous rugs, runners, and original fabric samples line the floor to form a multilayered surface as

Above A graphic motif has been painted onto the walls that, together with the artwork mounted onto it, forms a secondary piece. An 18th-century gilded gesso table displays a group of sculptures, from the "reclining figure" by Henry Moore to the plaster tortoises that Joe has made, which mix art pedigree with comedy.

At every juncture there are subtle reminders that the space, although home to an enviable collection of original art and furniture pieces, is permeated with an overriding sense of wit and irony. This is perfectly expressed by the life-size plastic ear clipped onto the grey wool curtains (formerly belonging to Eileen Gray) that separate the living area from the hallway.

interesting as the surrounding walls. Each area is composed as a "stand alone" vignette, forming a series of three-dimensional tableaus. The decoration was constructed free of the usual design principles, thus challenging perceptions of scale, proportion, and perspective, like a modern-day technicolored Escher.

Despite the density and intensity of the pieces, the lounge has an all-pervading air of cerebral calm. Every piece has its specific place and invariably forms a link to another element within the space. At first glance there seems to be no apparent link between the baroque gilded side table, the Todd Oldham painting *Fingernail Polish on Corkboard*, and the Mies van der Rohe white leather chair (accompanied by a micro-sized prototype of a Knoll armchair), all gathered around the metal "splat" coffee table. However, closer inspection reveals numerous connections of shape, colour, pattern, and form that link the space like a series of markers on a contour map. Museum-worthy pieces are placed with the same regard as flea-market finds, born of a refreshing egalitarianism that views pieces for their own merit rather than their perceived value. Circle and square motifs are found in some form on every surface, either overtly as a series of patterns or prints or covertly, referring back to a generic shape, form, or colour. Many possibilities of repeats, inversions, or reliefs appear on a variety of different substrates, ranging from wood and glass to fabric and plastic. Each version refers back to a larger original, providing continuity throughout the apartment like a recurring theme tune.

Below In this area of the lounge Joe plays with perspective and scale, taking great pleasure in placing the toy-sized Knoll sofa prototype below the large-scale painting by Mark Rothko. A blue velvet oblong frame is placed over layers of rugs and textiles on the floor to highlight them.

In the kitchen, the volume on the circle motif is turned up to crescendo level. Layer upon layer of patterned surfaces cover what Joe describes as "an ugly kitchen with uninteresting cabinets," transforming it into a three-dimensional painted interiorscape. The effect is like standing in the middle of a kaleidoscope, with each level of pattern building from a single colour outline, to a two-colour version, through to an overlapping three-colour version on every surface. Glass paint across the window and floor paint on the linoleum continues the pattern. As Joe says, "when in doubt, paint it out." The awkward dynamic of the kitchen space has been transformed into the visual equivalent of a Black Forest gateau with a definite cherry on top, further confirmed by the catwalk of cake tins at ceiling level which seem to be filing past overhead.

The master bedroom utilizes the circular motif in three colours: black, yellow, and white. Walls are faced with custom-designed and -built panels, which conceal wardrobes and are decorated with canary yellow inset sections, in turn, perforated to form a geometric block pattern. The ceiling is painted black with the structural supporting beams highlighted in white (the inverse of the

Above Left An Art Nouveau lamp base is transformed into a unique piece that spans 30 years of design history. Having replaced missing fittings with period ones, Joe found a 1950s textile that referred to the pattern within the base to use for the shade.

Below Left Walls, architraving, and floors are all blank canvases for decoration, according to Joe. Here the circular motif that runs throughout the entire apartment explores repeat versions, leaving no surface unadorned by this complex patterned layer.

ceiling treatment in the lounge), building on
the almost two-dimensional graphic quality
established by the walls. Side walls are
covered by hundreds of individual
postcards of the same abstract image,
mounted in overlapping rows with almost
scientific precision to create a secondary,
larger-patterned wall covering. The
postcard wall acts as a backdrop for
a collection of major artworks, lit by
a centrally hung, brass-and-Perspex
pendant uplighter, also perforated, and
surrounded by a dancing mobile of
Perspex snowflakes. The view from the
room into the hallway shows a section
of the circular pattern established in the
kitchen, but this time in the same three
colours found in the master bedroom. The
colours and motif form an instant visual
connection with the rest of the apartment.

For Joe, books seem to fill a place
beyond passion, forming the cornerstones
of his creative multidimensional essays.
They are to be found everywhere – above
eye level, behind sculptures, next to table
lamps, and lining the midnight-blue
horizontally striped walls leading to the
bathroom. The wall stripes lead the eye
to the bathroom, where they change
direction and become a vertical
accompaniment to the circular motif, now

Above Layer upon layer
of surfaces, all covered
in versions of the circular
motif, play with perspective
and perception in equal
measures. In the master
bedroom, the perforated
lemon yellow panels create
a three-dimensional pattern
to disguise the wardrobes.

Left Joe transformed the kitchen into a pattern fest, with at least four versions of the circular motif covering every surface, including the sash window and linoleum floor. At ceiling level, a floating procession of cake tins is strategically placed.

in black spots on candyfloss pink, which cover the bathtub. Hanging to either side of the bath are velvet drapes – Joe's neo-baroque take on a shower curtain – further emphasized by the painting, *Portrait of Lisa and Joe,* by Thomas Rowe hanging above. A pair of antique stone dogs, which seem to be supporting the white porcelain sink, are the signature on this Egypto-baroque effect. Although a bathroom, the space has been treated as any other, incorporating the washing apparatus into the scheme as one would a piece of furniture or an accessory.

The detail and design of the space has been deconstructed, challenging the general perceptions and parameters of interior design, and a totally resolved abstract synthesis of contrasts and contradictions has been created. Like a whirlwind tour, the apartment starts with the baroque ornateness of a Tsar's palace, continues through a Doris Day movie, goes to lunch with Warhol, and finishes with tea with Vasarely. It journeys through eras and environments in "cut and paste" form, alternately layering paint and pattern with passion. If, as Joe says about his design approach, "I don't want a room to be a one liner," then this apartment is definitely a space in deep conversation.

Right Circles take a back seat as lines dominate the bathroom, although the sugar pink bath is covered in an ermine-like rash of black spots. Claret drapes and a Rembrandtesque painting build on the regal theme, and two stone dogs guard the porcelain sink.

Georgian House
Hampstead
London
UK

Behind the early Georgian façade of what, at first glance, seems to be a traditional four-storey house in Hampstead, stands a glorious haven of eclecticism, created by owners Jacqueline and Steven Palmer. The couple found the house at the end of a two-year search, and fell in love with its position, proportions, and possibilities almost immediately. Jacqueline was attracted to the more contemporary aspects of the house, while Steve was drawn to the antique and historical atmosphere. Each found within the house the perfect platform to express their individual design tastes.

Inside, the architectural infrastructure fuses two contrasting elements: the historical and the contemporary. Square, high-ceilinged, elegant rooms, some still lined with the original panelling, contrast with the light-filled open-plan ground floor.

Although they were aware of the scale of the house before they moved, Jacqueline says, "we were shocked when we moved in because the house had previously been so highly furnished that it seemed smaller." Faced with a huge space to transform into a family home, they avoided the initial attraction of using a "professional designer." As Jacqueline explains, "We worried about having the space designed for us, fearing not being able to make our own stamp on the place and therefore not being able to connect with it. Ultimately we preferred to make our own choices."

So the creation of their home became a journey without a final destination – more of a random exploration of the couple's individual and shared tastes. Original pieces of furniture with a strong visual identity, collected from around the globe and very often born of a *coup de foudre* during a holiday, found their way to the London home. As a writer and poet, Jaqueline travels for inspiration, whereas Steven does so for business. On several occasions, "to extend the experience and bring it back home," Jacqueline has had pieces recreated that she could not bear to leave behind, often tracking down the original maker. The house is punctuated by examples of these rare pieces of

Right The pared-down minimalism of the first-floor "relaxation" area is lit by a combination of natural daylight, a reflective silver-painted ceiling, and a lamp by Isamu Noguchi. Muted 18th-century antiques accompany vibrant contemporary pieces.

international heritage, such as the replica of the hand-carved bed they slept on during their stay at Château Bagnols in France, which now stands in their bedroom. The electric blue velvet sofa in the study, is a copy of one that was first spotted in the bar of Hôtel Costes in Paris.

Sensing an overall lack of cohesion in the design of the interior, Jacqueline and Steven decided to consult a fung shui expert. They hoped that focusing on the more spiritual aspects of the house would enable them to find a framework that could unite all the stand-alone elements already established. However, the changes proposed were too numerous and disruptive to implement. Instead, they concentrated on several key elements that would alter the aesthetic of the house. This approach entailed painting the first-floor ceilings a metallic silver and installing several large wall-size mirrors with a liberal sprinkling of crystals and mirrored globes throughout. The changes enabled the couple to form a more personalized structure within which to develop.

One of the pivotal elements of fung shui – water – was reconciled with the giant fish tank, which doubles as a room divider between the lounge and kitchen on the ground floor. The fluid aquamarine

Above Left A detail of the 1970s "Sputnik" lamp, like a chrome-plated molecular explosion, lights the space with silvered bulbs and leaves a patterned speckled version of itself on surrounding surfaces.

Below Left The photo-printed inflatable cushion adds colour and texture to the matt surface of the moulded chair. The colour links the cushion with the green silk velvet upholstery of the gilded 18th-century sofa next to it.

glass block, speckled with darting splashes of neon colour, forms a natural patterned backdrop to the ultra-modern steel-and-glass kitchen on one side and the uber-eclectic lounge on the other. The

dining area is dominated by a hand-carved 18th-century wooden table – a "find in a Paris antique shop," which once belonged to the actress Sarah Bernhardt. Around it sits a multicoloured collection of

Above Hanging from the exposed oak beams of the master bedroom is the "Bubble" chair by Eero Aarnio. Alessandro Mendini's "Proust" armchair stands in the background. The hand-crafted bed is adorned by a collection of draped saris.

chairs, each one with a covetable design pedigree. Fluid aluminium forms with velvet upholstery accompany moulded plastic in primary colours. A "Sputnik" light hangs overhead. The lounge area is furnished with Italian contemporary sofas in navy blue, softened by the woven and fake fur throws and rugs placed around them. A high-tech media centre, which seems almost perfunctory, is understandable when on the facing wall an aluminium Marc Newson "Lockheed Lounge" chair stands like a suspended drop of mercury. A bank of glazed doors opens onto the exotic *son et lumière* garden outside.

The entrance hallway first introduces the Georgian elements of the house before revealing the contemporary part beyond. Adjacent to it is an intimate series of rooms, which play host to a miscellany of commissioned and collected pieces. A white fibreglass Eames chair, practically filling an entire wall and glowing against the dark panelling, dominates the room to the right of the entrance hall, which serves as the library. Next to the chair, in front of an exposed brick hearth, sits an 18th-century hand-carved armchair, upholstered in jewel-red silk damask. A richly patterned antique rug provides a visual connection between the furniture pieces. A series of

contemporary Italian table lamps and a string of red chilli lights illuminate the space, lending it a Rembrandt-like quality.

The amber glow of the panelling continues to the room on the left. A floor-standing "Sputnik" light is positioned next to the midnight-blue sofa, lined with brass studs and dramatic fringing. Another

Above An 18th-century Italian wardrobe fills one of the walls of Jacqueline's study. A circular polished wood table, laced with a dramatic grain, is used as a writing desk. Antonio Citterio's navy-and-white striped "T" swivel chair adds contemporary flavour.

Above The fluid lines of Charles and Ray Eames's 1948 white fibreglass chaise are highlighted by the dark oak panelling. The oversized brick Georgian hearth acts as a textural backdrop to the refined curves of the 18th-century gilded chair.

intricately patterned rug covers the original wood flooring, lightening the overall effect.

The winding wooden staircase lined in oak panelling connects the ground floor to the rest of the house. Although derived from a classical Georgian staging of intricate cornicing, high ceilings, and floor-

to-ceiling windows, the first floor has an almost loft-like flavour and exudes an air of contemporary calm. This modern-day Zen zone, with its silver ceilings, chalk-white walls, and stripped wooden floors has been designed as a relaxing, open-plan, spiritual space. This in-house retreat once again rejects the obvious for the original. No mats and spiritual icons adorn it; instead, an 18th-century hand-carved gilded sofa, upholstered in golden green silk velvet, sits next to a red round beanbag. A collection of sheepskin and woven rugs provides a series of textural stepping stones crossing the floor space.

The adjacent room is Jacqueline's average-sized study. The room is dominated by two dramatic large-scale pieces; one is a circular wooden table, laced with a dramatic woodgrain pattern, and the other is an antique floor-to-ceiling wardrobe. The table was hand-made by Jacqueline's grandfather, a master cabinet-maker. The wardrobe, an 18th-century Italian masterpiece, provides a historical backdrop to the highly contemporary "T" chair. Rather than making the space seem smaller, these scaled-up furniture pieces have lent a sense of history and continuity through their natural and handcrafted patterning.

The master bedroom is built into the void of the roof. The ceiling is covered by a network of exposed beams, which gives it an almost Tudor atmosphere. The ornately carved French four-poster bed stands on a geometrically patterned Pop Art rug. The huge micro-patterned "Proust" armchair

links the antique with the modern. Hanging by a chain, a 1960s "Bubble" chair spans the space like a giant magnifying glass.

Throughout the interior, the rooms play host to a random yet considered gathering of classic and contemporary pieces with little visual connection between them, other than a shared space. Each has been created in isolation, like a constellation of satellites on a launching pad. However, Jacqueline and Steven's individual and joint design tastes meld together within this early Georgian arena to create a distinctive home with a global flavour.

Below The deep-buttoned midnight-blue sofa by Jacques Garcia is trimmed with the extra-large twisted silk fringing that has become his signature. The "Sputnik" lamp's light patterns illuminate the oak panelling, casting a warm glow over the walls.

Surface

Surfaces provide the platform for colour, texture, and finish in the modern eclectic home. The combination of these elements, which meld to express personality and taste, leave an individual imprint on a space. Using surfaces as a starting point shifts the focus of a space to the more elemental infrastructure of floors and walls, providing the perfect opportunity for establishing external design parameters, which in turn support an inner identity. Surfaces provide the opportunity to address an interior in several varieties of scale, ranging from broad sweeps, which establish the atmosphere of the infrastructure of the space, through to surface finishes, which tend to focus on detail. The process very often alternating from one to another in the creation of a modern eclectic interior.

Surfaces provide structural tableaus that set the scene and establish spatial shifts between areas. They can remain in the background, providing a backdrop for additional decorative layers of self-expression, or they can dominate in the foreground as the focus of the space. Runs of uninterrupted surfaces delineate a space, establishing a series of areas and encouraging a sense of fluidity. By focusing on the reductive process

of taking a space back to its essence, "its four walls," the practical side of paring down and re-evaluating collected possessions can be a freeing experience. In a fast-paced consumerist world, going "back to basics" by eliminating the superfluous and retaining only a core collection of items with a personal significance can be deeply cathartic. In modernism, the elemental infrastructure is where the minimal interior ends; in modern eclecticism, it is where the creation of an interior begins.

Making a unique statement is paramount to the ethos of modern eclecticism, and surfaces offer the opportunity to explore a vast range of design possibilities. Whether surfaces are used to reconcile natural and synthetic elements or to provide a connection between internal and external spaces or interrelated areas, it is the alchemy of contrasting surfaces and finishes that plays a pivotal role. Surface finishes made of natural substrates are imbued with a resonance that links the natural world to a contemporary environment. Natural surfaces develop a patina, which evolves over time through age and wear and tear. They have a living, tactile quality, which synthetic surfaces try to emulate but

Above Left The surface finish of the matt white upholstered sofa corner unit contrasts with the earthy terracotta tones of the hand-baked tiles below. The arrangement creates a series of squares, from the grid-like tiles to the large forms of the furniture.

Above Right The smooth velvet pile of the midnight-blue sofa catches the light, accentuating the undulating surface of the piece. The sofa exudes an air of sensual luxury, with colours that move from soft Prussian blue to the inkiest of tones.

Below Left The nonreflective, textural quality of the concrete floor is further emphasized by the glossy smoothness of the wide inlaid marble bands. The design creates a "reversed out" effect of individual concrete tiles set into a marble framework.

Below Right This Far Eastern screen, inlaid with mother-of-pearl, once decorated an old hotel, but now forms the focal point of a bathroom. Inset into the window, it replaces an urban view with a backlit luminous panel, and establishes a soft palette.

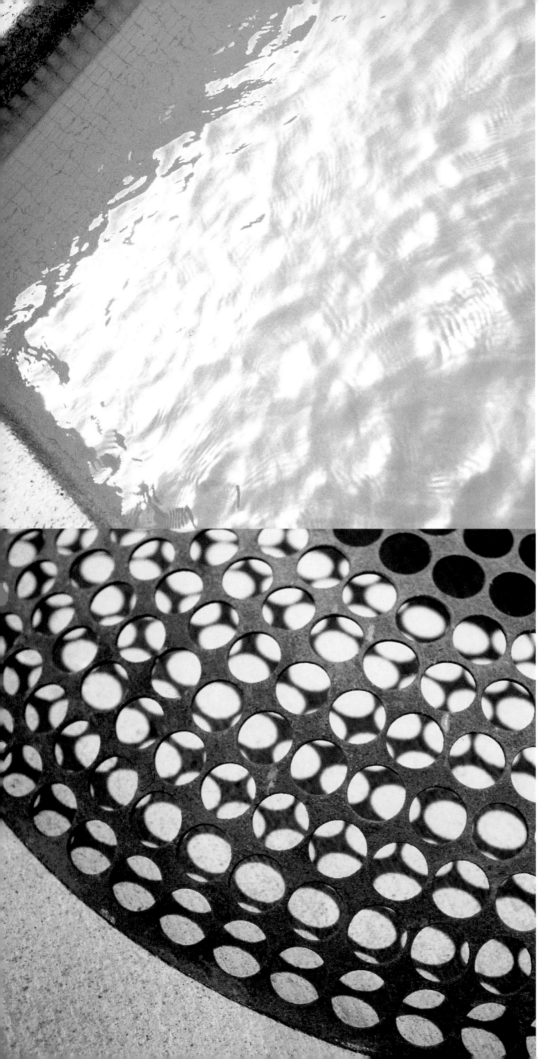

usually only achieve on a purely visual level. Surfaces made from natural materials, whether locally sourced or imported from further afield, provide a counterpoint to the constancy of synthetic surfaces in a contemporary interior. The subtle mixing of both natural and synthetic materials can be achieved by using a particular finish. For example, a reflective finish can achieve cohesion when a dramatically grained, highly polished marble, either underfoot or surface-mounted on a wall, provides a dramatic backdrop for a run of highly polished stainless steel units. A contrasting combination of textural finishes can also merge surfaces, such as in a space where a rough cement-rendered internal wall is lined by a row of tall natural bamboos that have been planted in a rectangle of soil inset into a plywood floor.

Playing with scale and distance can add an extra dimension to a surface. A panoramic vista encapsulated in a glass patio door or a reflection bouncing from an indoor pool onto the back of a sandblasted glass wall can create moving abstract wall-sized images. Such organization of surfaces brings movement and a mercurial element of progressive transformation to static, fixed surfaces.

Above Left The surface of the water in this mosaic-lined swimming pool ripples gently as the wind skims over it. Like an artwork of its own, the pool is a glistening aquamarine block inset into a textural geometric lawn.

Left The perforated-metal circular base of a contemporary nude sculpture is lit by a single ceiling-mounted spotlight. The circular cut-outs repeat in shadow form, creating a more complex secondary pattern.

Surfaces with inherent qualities, such as those particularly present in antique materials, can be further highlighted by cleverly juxtapositioning them with other, more contemporary, contrasting surfaces for a low-tech, high-impact statement. An antique hand-embroidered cushion placed on a contemporary leather armchair enables each piece to add value to the other. In the same way, two types of glass can build on each other's reflective yet translucent qualities, such as an organic fluid hand-blown sculptural form positioned on a simple glass console.

In the modern eclectic interior, the play of surface and finish provides the external structure that supports the inner lives of the inhabitants of the space. Surfaces work in two- and three-dimensional ways, establishing both the parameters of a space and the background and foreground of an interior; the final emphasis is modulated according to the required function and desired effect. In modern eclecticism, the mixing of contrasting finishes and the combining of surface textures are driven as much by desire and passion as by design. This approach provides a multidimensional opportunity to create an interior that is imbued with a personal dynamic.

Above The spiral steel staircase has pressed treads, which provide a decorative and functional nonslip surface. A bed of pebbles is inset into the wood floor, providing an organic counterpoint.

Overleaf Left The vertical lines of this glossy, veneered Formica breakfast chair, c.1950, introduce a subtly patterned surface to the smooth, neutral, linoleum floor.

Overleaf Right A detail of a bronze sculpture, which dominates the hallway a half-level above the lounge area, displays alternating textured and smooth surfaces.

Above Left A carved 18th-century, French, rose marble fireplace surrounds an enormous hearth. Its bold graphic lines contrast with the flame-red of the pigmented plaster walls.

Above Centre The lines and forms of this original art piece seem almost architectural. Minimal, white, three-dimensional surfaces throw hard-edged shadows, which further delineate the shapes.

Above Right A zebra-skin introduces pattern and texture to the parquet flooring. The wooden floor surface is laced with a woodgrain self-pattern, and its angular zigzag construction creates a secondary pattern.

Below Left The riven slate kitchen floor tiles are butted against a raised stainless steel inset strip, delineating the junction between the tiles and the adjacent wood flooring.

Below Centre The inset brass handles of this antique piece, formerly a lawyer's cabinet, contrast with the rubıne tones of the polished wood. The cabinet, now used as a sideboard, adds colour and a historical element to the dining area.

Below Right A detail of a beech dining table, designed by Frans van der Heyden as a part of his Birdman furniture collection, shows the unique and highly recognizable "crossed" wooden leg formation.

Contemporary House Islington London

Behind an unremarkable façade in a semi-industrial street on the outskirts of Islington in London stands a spectacular space. Hewn from a former disused match factory, this contemporary masterpiece is home to Richard and Rea Thomas. Richard, a high-profile hair stylist with a celebrity clientele, working very much in the public eye, and Rea, who uses her nursing expertise to work with disadvantaged children, synthesize two different personalities with contrasting tastes.

The couple found the match factory in a semi-converted state; all the architectural work had been completed, but nothing was finished or functioning. As Richard describes it, "it was very stagnant and tired." Having moved to London from a listed 17th-century stone manor house in an Oxfordshire village, the couple traded the detached for the derelict, but in the process had acquired an enormous space with even greater design potential.

Richard and Rea decided to work within the inherited architectural framework that had already been established by architects Paxton Locher. Into a series of modular interconnecting areas was space for an indoor pool and an exterior roof garden. With such a dynamic infrastructure to work around, the couple transformed the vast void in the course of a year into a metropolitan masterpiece.

They established their own "blueprint" for the space by reworking the layout to suit their particular requirements. On the ground floor a modular guest suite was created with a fully retracting partition wall, which could reconfigure the space into two bedrooms. Dominated by a mobile bed on wheels (with locks), which is covered by Mongolian lamb throws and a plethora of hand-woven antique cushions, the room has a bohemian atmosphere. A distressed leather armchair and a Persian rug reinforce the effect. An ornately gilded Georgian mirror, leaning against the far wall, is lit by a French 1920s floor-standing industrial lamp. The master bedroom incorporates a "floating bed," resting on top of a custom-built, steel-and-walnut, walk-in wardrobe,

Right Sandblasted glass panels, which separate the pool from the living area, have a cool minimalism. White low-slung sofas and a Finnish modern classic armchair and footstool sit next to Balinese tables. The space is lit by Philippe Starck lamps.

Above The triple-height atrium above the staircase provides an exhibition space for a collection of antique hand-carved mirrors, original sculptural pieces, and modern art. A glass orb table light sits on a sixteenth-century coffer, spattering the wall behind with refracting patterns.

a half-level below, so creating a double-height mezzanine level within the space.

The sleeping and bathing areas are linked by a long minimal corridor, which runs across the central half landing on the first floor and connects the enclosed wooden staircase that faces the entrance with the rest of the space. A handrail, made of polished steel rods, equidistantly ranged between the steel uprights that anchor them, lines the stairs up to the next level. A glance upward reveals an extraordinary expanse of space that is simply breathtaking. This industrially

proportioned arena, intersected by a series of elemental planes and surfaces, provides a contemporary canvas for the open-plan kitchen, dining, and living areas that form the home.

Lining the entire length of one wall, a series of warehouse-style windows flood the space with natural daylight. On the opposite wall, and mirroring the proportions of the windows, is a series of huge sandblasted glass panels, which underline the inherent minimalism of the architecture and hint at the space beyond – the heated indoor pool. This particular

pool is a temple to minimalism and
has been designed using reductionist
principles – the idea being to solely
contain the water. The introduction of
an area dedicated to water contained
within an elemental space adds an
almost spiritual layer of calm to the interior.
The run of water, cut out of a floor area
of the same size with a walkway on one
side only, and the huge sandblasted
planes of glass, framing the other side
and flooding the space with a diffused
light, create a "pure" space," free of
distraction. Apart from the element of
"uber luxury" that a heated indoor pool
provides, it is also a space of pure
escape from the stresses of urban life.
The ability to escape into a more
spiritual level is a key element for Richard
and Rea, and forms the cornerstone of
their life philosophy.

Rather than continue the minimalist
ethos established by the architecture of
the building, Richard and Rea adopted
a much more personal approach for the
interior. Rea's belief that "a home should
support your sense of being" by forming
a connection between "your interior and
the interior" is expressed in the diverse
collection of individual pieces, which
form a narrative throughout the space.

Above Right The Dutch
leather "Castor" chair has a
matching footstool, which
doubles as a low side table.
The tapestry cushion
introduces texture to the
smooth leather upholstery.

Right A collection of
antique pewter platters,
with surfaces pitted
through years of use,
seems to emerge from the
stainless steel worktop
underneath.

Above The dramatic metal nude with spiky hair and a perforated circular base was bought by Richard and Rea in Dublin. It visually introduces the swimming pool, which is contained within the glass panels behind the sculpture.

Interestingly, it is the raw elements, such as the rough stone steps that lead up to the pool level from the dining area, that establish Rea's essential connection with the space. Despite their contemporary context, the steps remind Rea "of a castle with big steps and high walls." Her passion for all things historical, particularly the medieval and early Tudor eras, is expressed in the religious and ethnic iconography that decorates her home, with antique textiles adding a textural layer to the minimal surfaces underneath. Richard's design sensibilities, on the

other hand, are allied more closely with 20th-century design classics, but allow room for both the baronial and the baroque to feature.

Expanding on the marriage of influences throughout the interior, Rea says, "It is exactly the differences that we bring to our relationship that are expressed in our choice of pieces. It is these differences between us that are essential. For us it is definitely opposites that attract." Translated into the creation of the interior, this has been very much a joint process. Richard adds, "I never buy anything without Rea…"

Addressing the change of scale, and trying to keep the number of pieces down to a minimum, Richard and Rea retained only the "large, substantial, and generous pieces" from their previous house, choosing to sell many of the pieces they had accumulated over the years. For them, this process proved to be quite cathartic. Other pieces have been introduced into the space, such as the 17th-century hand-carved wooden chandelier of Spanish origin, which had been bought years ago "without any where to hang it" and which now hangs above the antique dining table. Facing the almost baronial dining area is a polished stainless steel kitchen that takes the concept of dramatic juxtapositioning to the extreme. However, the whole effect is softened through the introduction of a length of warm grey marble that delineates the perimeter of the open-plan area while doubling as a work surface/bartop. Reflective surfaces act as a neutral visual link between the stone steps, crowned by a contemporary bronze sculpture set against the backdrop of sandblasted glass, the starkly modern stairwell, lined with gilt-framed Renaissance miniatures, and the living area beyond.

At first glance, the living area, defined by a series of set pieces, seems sparsely furnished, even minimal, yet has an overriding sense of calm and openness. A vast expanse of light woodstrip flooring gives the space tonal warmth, lending it an almost Far Eastern atmosphere. A pair of deep, oversized, pure white sofas are filled with a collection of richly embroidered and woven antique velvet cushions, encouraging "a long-term stay." Picking up on the Oriental theme, a group of low, hand-carved, Balinese tables act, collectively, as a coffee table. Placed around the central sofas are pieces of furniture, ranging from original latter 20th century design classics to witty contemporary "one-offs."

A contemporary fireplace is cut out of the starkly white end wall. Above it hangs a gilded and painted Gothic triptych, which would not look out of place in a medieval house of worship, but which also looks remarkably at home here. The walls on either side of the chimneybreast seem to be underlined by a graphic system of glass shelving. Held in place by a series of almost invisible tension wires, the shelving was inspired by a system the couple had seen used for a retail display. The living area is lined on both sides by glass panels, and seems to float in between,

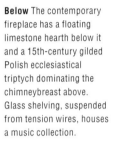

Below The contemporary fireplace has a floating limestone hearth below it and a 15th-century gilded Polish ecclesiastical triptych dominating the chimneybreast above. Glass shelving, suspended from tension wires, houses a music collection.

being grounded only by the large-scale, antique, dark wood furniture that lends a sense of history and continuity. The wall of windows that frames the space divides the surrounding natural views into grid-like sections and is left mercifully free of any covering or decoration. As Rea says, "blowing leaves are the best window treatment in the world." The windows, along with the sandblasted radiators, maintain the clean, minimal lines.

Richard and Rea share a sensibility and spirituality that is best expressed in the creation of their roof garden, a lush,

exotic, verdant expanse built around Zen principles. The roof garden is framed on one side by the glass panels of the pool below and on the other side by a panoramic London skyline. The glass panels are rendered opaque from a combination of the sandblasting on one side and the mist from the steaming pool below, adding to the ethereal quality of this inner London Eden. Like a fluorescent magic carpet floating above the rooftops, this organic layer crowns the couple's contemporary kingdom, where their "home is their castle."

Modernist House Spain

Casa Carlhian, named after and built for its owner, Marguerite Marie Carlhian, is a modernist villa designed in 1983 by celebrated Spanish architect Josep Pratmarso. Crowning the pinnacle of a hill and surrounded by the Pyrenees mountains, it overlooks an uninterrupted panorama of the northern Spanish coastline. The villa is one of the best examples of the architect's ability to fuse the natural with the constructed.

Originally designed in an abstract way as a series of spaces, Casa Carlhian is imbued with a defining modernism that transcends time. Continuous planes and surfaces that barely touch are humanized by using such local materials as honey-toned tiles and dramatically grained woods. The house has been designed to reflect a seamless flow from the exterior to the interior, with nature almost seeming to form the outside walls.

Marguerite commissioned Casa Carlhian to be built as a holiday villa in which to escape the Parisian winter chill, but it is now where she spends most of her time. Marguerite worked closely with Pratmarso, her style being even more minimalist than his, to create her "floating dream house." Although a skilled draughtsman, Pratmarso found the production of plans and elevations "halted the creative process" and preferred to work in a more abstract fashion, producing sketches and often aquarelles to show his clients. With a background as a fine artist, he designs houses in the way an abstract artist would paint a canvas – with broad sweeps of the brush, thereby leaving the viewer to provide the detail. Translated into architectural form this meant that Pratmarso created a sense of volume and surface before addressing the technical infrastructure of the space. Natural light plays a key role in his designs, informing every aspect of the forms that he creates.

Exterior walls, almost apologetic of their presence, are rendered transparent by the insertion of enormous glass windows and doors, which let the breathtaking vistas form a natural perimeter to the interior. Planes are white,

Right The dining room reinforces the Oriental theme. Vivid orange walls provide the perfect backdrop for a Japanese paper pendent light, a black lacquer table, and Gio Ponti chairs. Bamboo blinds and tatami floor mats give the room an air of privacy.

Below The almost monochromatic decor of the white Cassina corner sofa and the white walls is warmed by the terracotta floor tiles. Huge abstract canvases, one in black by Luis Tomasello and the other in white by Leopoldo Novoa, accompany dramatic bronze sculptures.

lateral, and elongated, resonating with a timeless modernism. Walls of oversized, rough, asymmetrical stones, excavated from the land surrounding the site, are juxtaposed with floors made of locally produced, handcrafted tiles. The ochre patina of the flooring refers visually to the field of giant sunflowers outside, which tower over the roof at the side of the villa and bob in the reflection of the aquamarine swimming pool. Rather than constructing a flat roof, continuing the elemental ethos of the white exterior walls, Pratmarso designed a terracotta-tiled pitched roof.

The tiles were hand-made and baked in local ovens, and form a visual connection with the style of neighbouring farmhouses.

Although the villa is not essentially a big house, inside the space is imbued with a sense of openness and cohesion. A series of low and retracting walls define spaces and create areas that flow into one another. The living area is framed on either side by simple, white, upholstered, low-slung corner units from the 1970s, their shape further highlighted by graphically placed avocado-green scatter cushions. One corner of the sofa unit rests against

a low internal wall that leads the eye to the hallway behind. In a recessed area, situated at the back of the lounge, a study area and fireplace are personalized with a collection of Marguerite's family photographs and ornaments, randomly placed around the space. A picture window above forms a "seasonal tableau," as Marguerite describes it. An antique bamboo card table, next to the wall-size glass sliding doors that lead to the terrace outside, introduces the Oriental theme that features repeatedly throughout the house. A bank of simply hung, bleached cotton

drill drapes form a pleated background to two ladder-backed chairs, which recall Van Gogh's *My Bedroom in Arles, 1889.* A collection of large monochromatic modern art hangs on the chalk-white walls that frame the lounge, providing a counterpoint to the pure fluid lines of the interior. Marguerite's substantial collection of unique 20th-century artworks, which are mostly abstract and very often monotoned with some form of self-textural layer, play a pivotal role in establishing the atmosphere of this high-end modernist interiorscape. At first glance these

Above The terrace, paved in terracotta, lines the length of the house and is bordered by a manicured lawn that overlooks the panoramic view below. Central to the exterior space are table and benches bought in Girona. Two leather-and-wood folding chairs, c.1960, sit at either end of the table, which itself is decorated with Italian glassware.

large-scale works operate on a purely decorative level, by introducing dramatic planes of solid tone and texture to the elemental white walls. However, closer inspection reveals a series of artworks operating on an almost allegorical level, which represent, albeit in abstracted form, "life." With subject matter ranging from war to the celebration of life, these artworks, together, lend the interior an echo of history – a global sense of the world translated through art pieces into an accessible format.

Adding a circular motif to this angular haven, a floor lamp with a round Japanese paper shade, similar to the pendant versions still being manufactured today, sits on top of a black wrought-iron stand made locally for Marguerite, successfully marrying the retro with the Eastern. Several further pieces in wrought iron, some by renowned artists commissioned by Marguerite and others rare antiques, such as the 12th-century Japanese tambour used to collect rainwater, punctuate the living area. Large abstract paintings in black and white reinforce the minimal colour theme and angular shapes. Collectively the pieces represent Marguerite's passion for, and extensive knowledge of, fine art and rare antiques.

Above Left An iron sculpture by artist Pablo Reinoso, which fills the corner of the dining room, is here shown in detail. Its form, reminiscent of a tribal shield, contrasts with the bamboo blinds and orange walls around it.

Below Left Changing light and shadows play along the corridor where this painting by Luis Tomasello is wall-mounted to face a window. The three-dimensional aspects of the painting's cuboid forms alter according to the light.

The hallway, a half-level up from the living area, links the main entrance to the rest of the house. At one end a light, square, spacious entrance hall with a double-width glass door leads to an internal courtyard, which is dominated by a graphic bronze sculpture. Glass continues as a motif inside, with a collection of variously sized, vividly coloured, Murano-glass organic shell forms resting on the heavy glass console table next to the entrance door. Leading off the hallway are the kitchen and dining rooms, the latter providing a rare splash of intense colour among the overriding neutral interior tones. The dining room walls, decorated in rich orange tones, lend the room a warm intimacy. The black lacquer dining table and chairs, placed on a large tatami floor mat and framed by long, backlit, bamboo blinds, give the space an Oriental flavour, further highlighted by the paper pendant light and the lacquer-framed Japanese prints on the walls.

At the opposite end of the hallway is the sleeping area, strategically separated from the living and eating areas. The main bedroom returns to the calm, white palette

Below The master bedroom has been decorated in neutral tones, which allow the colourful exterior landscape (on view through the glass doors) to set the scene. An iron sculpture by Pablo Reinoso shares an economy of line with the painting by Henry Closon hanging above the desk.

Above An original medieval hand-painted Japanese art piece, featuring two paper birds, hangs above the bed. The rich tones of the painting are continued in the bedside tables and the antique carved Spanish wardrobe on the right.

used throughout the space. Dominated by large glass sliding doors on two sides, with views onto the terrace and garden that stretch to the panoramic horizon of the sea beyond, the room seems to have no defining boundaries between the natural exterior and the created interior.

Marguerite furnished the interior of the bedroom minimally, using a blend of several shades of white and introducing subtle gold and bronze tones in the form of an organic bronze-and-wood sculpture, a retro black leather chair, and a Japanese painting hung above the bed. The painting,

an original 12th-century hand-painted ceiling panel, was rescued from a derelict Japanese palace by a friend of Marguerite's. It was given to her as a gift, and is one of her most treasured pieces. Cotton canvas drapes from Paris hang simply in front of large picture windows, and can be drawn to provide privacy or opened to give an uninterrupted outdoor view. A carved antique wardrobe anchors the space and mirrors the deep tones of the writing desk on the opposite wall.

Outside, the terrace runs the length of the house, covered by a stone flat-roofed canopy made up of a configuration of two intersecting sections. The canopy provides shade throughout the day, while emphasizing the lateral lines of the terraced area below. Designed as an exterior open space without walls, the terrace seems to flow effortlessly from the interiorscape to the exterior landscape. The floor of the terrace is covered with large, locally produced, terracotta slabs, which are abutted to a graphic, manicured lawn. Inset into the tiled surround, the grass has a carpet-like quality that again refers to the fusion of the exterior with the interior. The long, uneven wooden table and accompanying benches are headed by two antique leather recliners. The table, formerly housed in a local monastery, has traded cloistered silence for gregarious socializing, and it now forms the centrepiece for Marguerite's outdoor living and entertaining.

Further along the terrace and adjacent to the pool, another socializing area is arranged around low-slung, contemporary, woven-cane chairs on black metal frames. A collection of small square tables, made from the same materials, double as additional seating. The pool, a turquoise aquatic length cut into a sleek smooth lawn, continues the elemental ethos.

More a space than a house, the villa is a fusion of planes and surfaces that achieve the perfect partnership between the natural and the constructed. With its own unique style it expresses the architect's philosophy "that any architecture which is in rapport with nature will never have to rely on fashion…" Using a design language formed from a natural alphabet, the surrounding land and seascapes provide an ever-changing context for this perfectly resolved exercise in elemental design, and for Marguerite it is her "space for all seasons."

Below A simple wooden bench stands in front of the tiled entrance to the house. The space is guarded by a 12th-century Thai bird sculpture, carved from a single piece of wood. Originally decorated with precious jewels, the bird is a traditional good luck charm.

Shape &
Form

Shape and form provide the plotting points of an interior. They establish the dynamic of a space by providing a framework of contours, like using broad brush strokes in preparation for the application of detail. Shapes punctuate the physical environment, helping to establish a visual language for the interior. Bold forms plot a visual story line, while contrasting shapes form a three-dimensional subtext. The key elements of shape and form can be divided into three layers: primary, which refers to the architectural infrastructure; secondary, which focuses on the shapes and forms of the furniture pieces themselves and their configuration in the interior; and tertiary, which highlights the decorative detail provided by accessories such as displayed objects, soft furnishings and wall decorations. The emphasis and importance placed on each of these elements will determine the overriding atmosphere of an interior.

In modern eclecticism, basic forms can be used to introduce a subtle level of cohesion. For example, the repetition of a particular visual idea can provide a link that connects diverse eras and styles. Alternatively, using a limited textural or colour palette can establish continuity among a variety of shapes and forms. The sequence and juxtapositioning of form and shape, whether free-standing or part of the architectural infrastructure, determines the inherent characteristics of an interior space.

In a modern eclectic interior, as in other more minimal environments, open-plan spaces inspire a seamless flow of activities from one area to another without formal division. Whether within an industrial loft conversion or inset into a more traditional context, merging spaces are imbued with a sense of fluid progression. The key to establishing focal points within an open-plan environment is the positioning of furniture. Whether performing a decorative or functional role, or a combination of the two, the shape, positioning, and subsequent configuration of the core furniture pieces will establish, on a practical level, the circulation routes from one area to the next and, on an emotional level, the atmosphere of the space. Acting as a subliminal index to the personality of the space, shape can be used to announce the function of a room, establishing whether it is public or private, formal or informal. Areas of enclosures provide privacy and open spaces announce access.

Above Left A detail of an iron tabletop sculpture, built around two straight uprights, displays its interlinking pieces. The sculpture was a rare find in a flea market on the outskirts of Munich.

Above Right An antique gilt-edged chair, one of a pair, has been upholstered in black silk moiré, giving this inherently classic piece a contemporary twist.

Below Left The spiralling iron sculpture was hand-formed by local Catalan craftsmen for artist Izabella Leszczynska. The crystal orb perched in its centre holds a curved reflection of its surroundings.

Below Right An antique Japanese good luck charm, hand-carved in wood with its surface pitted from years of handling, is placed at the foot of steps to protect the house and its inhabitants.

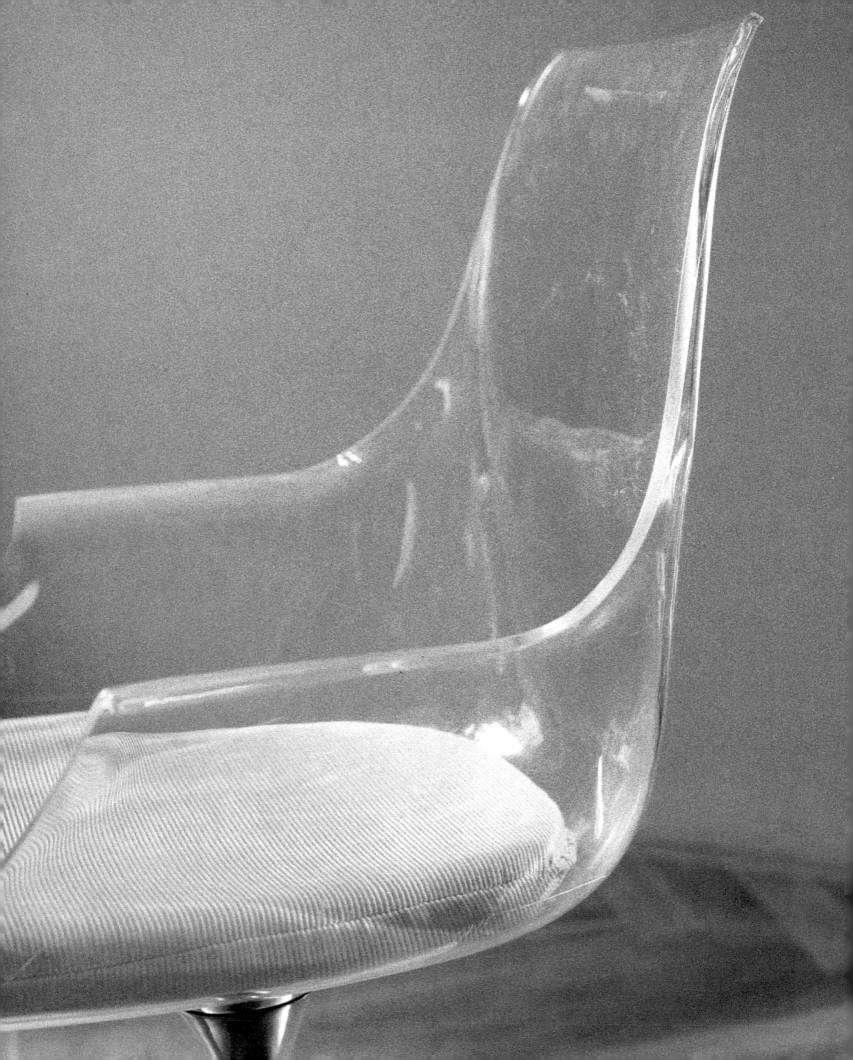

Above The exquisite carved detailing on this gilt Georgian mirror is further highlighted by its contrast to the starkly contemporary architecture of its surroundings.

Page 118 The distinctive curved wooden arms of an Eames chair contrast with the dark oak panelling that lines the walls of the bedroom, formerly the postmaster general's office.

Page 119 Original 1950s glassware from Poland has an organic form and inherent translucent quality that refers to the natural plant and sea life of its Catalan surroundings.

Shapes, in particular, establish visual punctuation points and can be used to form a more linear cohesive statement by all subscribing to the same type of group – for example, organic, cuboid, or curved. Shapes can also be used to introduce disparate and contrasting elements that provide a more random route through an interior.

Light reveals shape, form, and surface finish. Diffused light emphasizes the textural qualities of a form, while a sharp light highlights overall shape. Light also reveals the inherent personality and

character of a space by spotlighting the key forms that establish the pace of the space. Whether energized or languid, static or modular, each area is ascribed with its own unique atmosphere. Fluid curvaceous forms in a modern eclectic context may have hard surface textures, which natural or artificial lighting can highlight or diffuse, thus shifting the emphasis and balance of the space. By contrast, a formal piece of antique furniture, upholstered in a smooth-piled, vibrantly coloured velvet and washed with natural daylight, can scream "soft modern" in such a setting. However, place the same piece of upholstered furniture under the direct light of a tungsten spotlight, and its formal contours can override its surface finish, thus highlighting the antique heritage of the piece.

The creative transformation of a space into a modern eclectic interior can be driven by a passion for a particular design movement, a shape, a decorative motif, or a combination of several of these components. Elements of shape and form can be interwoven to combine old and new – the industrial with the historical, the antique with the contemporary, or the retro with the avant-garde. By relishing the insertion of unfamiliar materials into a domestic context, the infinite combinations of contrasting shapes and forms can create a personalized three-dimensional aesthetic statement. A healthy irreverence for established principles of interior design, such as scale, balance, and proportion, coupled with equal measures of inspiration and irony, will encourage the unexpected juxtapositioning of shape, form, and function that creates the modern eclectic interior.

Previous Page Left The fluid contours of a retro "no name" Perspex "Tulip" chair hold a beige corduroy cushion, which adds comfort without detracting from the piece's "lightness of being."

Previous Page Right A 1960s metal pendant light, reminiscent of a series of multicoloured chimes, hangs in front of an aluminium venetian blind, adding form and colour to a neutral bathroom.

Below This retro glassware, with its gently undulating random curves, forms part of a modular collection where each glass piece fits into the curves of the next piece, together forming a giant transparent vessel.

Above Left The diminishing curves of this wooden lampshade turn into a glowing burnt sienna spiral when lit. The backlit woodgrain forms a linear pattern on the surface.

Above Centre An ornate antique Murano chandelier, here shown in detail, reminded the owner of her Italian ancestry and the décor of her childhood. The piece has now been transplanted into her home in downtown Manhattan.

Above Right Shadows turn the graphic fluidity of a white fibreglass chaise by Charles and Ray Eames, c.1948, into a dramatic piece. The contrasting moody tones of the piece almost merge into the dark oak-panelled wall behind.

Below Left The mustard-coloured felted wool upholstery of a footstool and the bouclé woollen weave of the carpet add warmth and texture to the cool blue tones created by natural daylight flooding this roof-level extension.

Below Centre The concentric glass circles of a tall contemporary vase by Danny Lane have an organic quality that complements the spiralling curves of the Murano glass chandelier overhead.

Below Right A pair of original 1960s wall-mounted chrome lights are designed to be used with silvered mirror bulbs. When lit at night, the bulbs take on the vibrant tones of the lights' orange interior, throwing the exterior into shadow.

Purpose-built Apartment Munich Germany

On the top floor of a 1950s purpose-built block in a Munich suburb, gallery owners Carolin and Robert Stephan have created a sleek, ever-changing, yet honed, interior, using a diverse mixture of found, considered, and collected pieces, each of which has personal meaning for them.

Design at its most eclectic, from fashion to furniture, has been a continuous and shared passion for Carolin and Robert since they first met at university, despite the fact that both studied business administration and economics. "Robert's passion for design came first… his taste is more straight; mine a little more ironic," says Carolin, "yet together we are truly eclectic." Robert adds, "I ground Carolin and she pushes me further." Robert's taste is firmly rooted in the 20th century, spanning Art Deco and Eileen Gray through to Charles Eames, George Nelson, Michael Young, Jasper Morrison,

and Marc Newson. Carolin shares Robert's interest in the Art Deco movement, but it is the 1960s and 1970s that she adores.

In 1999 they opened their gallery, called *Eileen: Boutique for Eclectic Living*, in the centre of Munich. The couple decided to name the boutique after their daughter, because she was the catalyst for Carolin to change direction and open the gallery the couple had wanted for years. As Carolin explains, "without Eileen we would not have a gallery. I would still be working in fashion…"

Both at home and in their gallery the couple's design approach is to mix "high-style designer pieces" with "no name" items, creating a unique and surprisingly cohesive style of their own. They restock and redesign their gallery every two weeks so that the space is an ever-changing "living" room, designed around an eclectic collection of new and retro pieces. At weekends the gallery is as much "a social space as a showcase." At home, their lounge is often used as an extension of the gallery, and seems to act as a long- or short-stay parking space for newly acquired and rotating furniture and accessory pieces. There is a constant flow of objects

Right A huge photo-print of Brigitte Bardot and Gunter Sachs establishes the colour palette for the lounge. The black Jasper Morrison sofa came from Robert's previous flat and the Eames lounger, upholstered in cream leather, is one of a pair.

Left The dining room, painted in a soft Wedgwood blue, is lit by a collection of "one off" lights. The brass 1960s pendant light continues the honey tones of the original parquet floor and lights the Eero Saarinen dining table. A collection of "no name" retro chairs are dotted around the table.

between their gallery and their home, although the core pieces that define each room are permanent.

The lounge is dominated by a huge, unframed, grainy, duotone photo-print of newlyweds Brigitte Bardot and Gunter Sachs in a Lear jet, setting the tone for the interior by establishing a monochromatic background to the space. Intrigued by the story behind this rare shot of these world-famous icons, Carolin explained to me, "when I was still working at Hugo Boss, we had designed a collection inspired by Gunter Sachs and were looking for an image to encapsulate the new range. I found this picture of him with Brigitte Bardot – just married – in a vintage archive and had it enlarged for the in-store window display. When I left the company to open our gallery, I had become so attached to the image that I couldn't bear to leave it behind, so I asked if I could have the print. It was the first piece we hung in our new gallery and it literally stopped traffic. Everyone wanted it!"

The polished amber-toned floor is the original parquet, laid in a large geometric design throughout the apartment. It was discovered preserved in near-perfect condition under the fitted carpets left by the previous owners. Sprawled in the

middle of the glossy lounge floor lies a zebra-skin, hunted down by Robert in a local flea market. Placed around the skin is a collection of design classics that almost travel through time – from the Le Corbusier armchairs at one end of the room, through the beige-and-brown leather Eames loungers lining the wall, to the black Jasper Morrison sofa at the opposite end of the space. Like the members of an extended design family, each piece has a significance and resonance for Carolin and Robert. Together these pieces create a considered

Above The parquet-lined hallway has a wall-sized mirror along one wall, which gives the illusion of greater width. Reflected in the mirror is one of Philippe Starck's early chairs. Carolin's enviable bag collection is displayed on a 1960s chrome hanging rack with Perspex hangers.

and surprisingly contemporary interiorscape, imbued both with the history of their acquisition and with their newly designated role to play in the space.

A mixture of unique table and standard lamps from the 1960s and '70s lights the lounge. The only fixed lighting are a couple of original Italian spotlights from the 1980s and a matching pair of 1970s silver-and-orange wall-mounted tube lights, which frame the slimline 21st-century CD player sited between them like a picture. Below, a pair of Perspex cubes seems to almost float under the beige corduroy cushions of the ottomans on either side of the opening to the dining room.

The muted palette of the interior intensifies in the dining room, where the walls are painted in a very particular shade of blue. Almost Wedgwood-like, Carolin and Robert saw the particular tone of blue in a magazine but found that the paint that they had mixed to match resembled a sky blue colour when dry. So they began to layer grey tones on top of the blue base until they had recreated the colour from the magazine cutting. The result is an intensely saturated yet gentle blue that provides the perfect background for the chrome, gold, and beige tones of the furniture and accessories. On one side of

Above Left A rare example of a cased-and-cast Murano glass vase is one of a pair found by Robert and Carolin in two separate flea markets. The surface refracts in the natural daylight, highlighting its plum, heather, and amethyst tones.

Below Left The orange glass-and-chrome shades of this pendant light, c.1968, hanging from the ceiling, add some spot colour to the generic neutrally decorated kitchen. A considered collection of retro accessories fills the space.

the room, a long, white, metal-and-glass sideboard with chrome trim lines the wall. Originally it was an office storage system, but now holds a collection of retro glassware, rather than software. The dining table, an original Eero Saarinen, was bought in a private sale listed in a local newspaper advertisement. The "no name" chairs, still covered in the original gold corduroy, were found in a local flea market. The Perspex Saarinen-style "Tulip" chair on a stainless steel base, one of a pair, is mixed in with the other set of chairs to introduce a more random element to the interior. A diverse fusion of styles and eras light the space, from the original chrome Knoll table light with a glossy backlit blue shade to the 1980s cone-shaped floor-standing Italian uplighter from Robert's previous apartment. The windows are simply dressed in soft blue floor-to-ceiling linen curtains. In front of them and hanging above the dining table hangs another local flea-market find, a gold metal pendant light, c.1960. Against the opposite wall rests a glass coffee table, inlaid with onyx and lit by an internal light, making it look as if it had just finished residency on a James Bond film set. Above it, a large square gold panel mounted with six black horn-shaped vases recalls an early

Philippe Starck design moment. As Robert explained, "I first saw it in the window of a large department store in the centre of Munich at the time when Philippe Starck had just opened the Royalton. It was a piece of window display designed in the style Starck used in the Royalton and created by the store to promote these vases. I so loved it that I contacted the display manager and asked if I could buy it, and since then this piece has featured in every place that I have lived."

The long hallway runs through the apartment, connecting the rooms.

Below The 1970s Knoll chrome table lamp has a smoked charcoal plastic shade. A Danish grey leather "Tulip" chair was a find from an antique dealer in Munich. Against the wall, a glass-topped coffee table, inlaid with Perspex and onyx, has a glowing interior light source.

It showcases a collection of Carolin and Robert's most treasured "design and designer finds," such as the wall-mounted chrome-and-white plastic hanging rack, from which hangs a rubber Chanel bucket bag and a retro lizard handbag. Below it, against the wall, a 1970s swivel chair, upholstered in a floral fabric, recalls the fashion of that period. Opposite a wall-size mirror, which serves to widen the hallway, is an original Philippe Stark wooden chair – one of Robert's "first major investment purchases from my former life, before Carolin." The retro pendant light was bought from a local antique dealer for their gallery, but never found its way there, making the hallway its permanent home.

Eileen, their young daughter, has grown up surrounded by eclecticism. Her room is the only other space with coloured walls, painted in a buttercup yellow that was inspired by the circular rug they had bought before she was born. The walls and matching drapes warm the blue northern tones of natural daylight that flood the space. Her room is filled with mini designer furniture, with a variety of small-scale Verner Panton and Eames -style chairs to sit on and a pair of Philippe Starck asymmetrical sofas on which to lounge – all lit by a 1950s multicoloured Murano-glass pendant light, which hangs next to a glass mobile in the same colours.The room takes the concept of a playroom to a new design-led dimension, while retaining its inherent sense of fun.

Carolin and Robert's bedroom reverts back to the more monochromatic palette established in the living area. Chalk white walls are softened by the bespoke cherrywood bed, which they designed, and original parquet flooring underfoot. A Tom Dixon starlight hangs overhead. An original 1950s German-made wooden desk refers back to the Eames style, so

Below A micro collection of late 20th-century designer classics furnishes Carolin and Robert's daughter's bedroom. A Starck sofa and armchair provide adult seating, while the Verner Panton and baby Eames-style chairs offer perfect tea party furniture.

prevalent of the era. In front of the desk a smoked brown Perspex 1950s Gio Ponti-style chair takes pride of place. The story behind the acquisition of this chair illustrates Robert's continuous passion for collecting design classics. Spotted in the window of a local antique dealer during a recent holiday in Italy, the chair was bought by Robert, but would not fit into their already over-full car. One of a matching pair, the dealer agreed to deliver the chairs to Austria, which entailed an overnight journey of 320 kilometres (200 miles) for Robert, and where, on a designated bridge, he collected the chairs and drove them back to Munich.

With the dedication to the pursuit of good design, rather than purely famous design, playing a pivotal role in their lives, Carolin and Robert have created an interior that expresses their own individual style. Through the focused mixing of different styles – the old with the new, "no names" with design icons – there is nothing within their home that is superfluous. Every piece is a carefully considered addition to a space that is orchestrated by a signature tune of eclecticism. Uniform modernity is replaced with the space's own inherent identity, achieved by adopting the design philosophy that "less is definitely more."

Above Right A white, almost matt, smooth, egg-like retro table starkly contrasts with the Cubist painting by German artist Ida Baeder Buechel, a student of Fernand Léger; Buechel later went on to design wallpapers.

Below Right Shown here is a detail of the Philippe Starck-inspired window display that Robert bought from a department store in Munich, and which now hangs in the dining room. The display was a homage to the Royalton hotel in New York.

Interior-designed Triplex Manhattan New York

Located on the upper levels of a former disused warehouse on the lower West Side of Manhattan is a loft apartment spanning two internal floors, with the third and uppermost level built onto the roof. Interior designers to the celebrities, Michael Pierce and DD Allen, who together form the practice Pierce Allen, have worked closely with owner Jo Ellin Comerford to create a part-Modern, part-Miami triplex that successfully merges the industrial with the interior-designed.

The building is situated in the heart of one of the more cutting edge areas of Manhattan. Since the 1960s, when its commercial tenants left, the warehouse has been home to writers, artists, and musicians. Groups of those in the arts formed the early co-ops that converted the brownfield areas into vibrant alternative residential areas, which now form the cornerstone of the art world's subculture.

The loft apartments are accessed through the stripped heavy steel door of the main entrance to the building, once the loading bay of the warehouse. White-painted brick walls line the stone communal stairway, which accompanies the steel-clad lift (elevator). Huge galvanized steel pipes hiss and steam overhead, reminiscent of the engine room of an ocean liner. In true warehouse style, the lift door opens directly into the apartment. Once inside, the panoramic views of New York rooftops define the space, flooding every one of the windows with aerial views that must classify as a cinematographer's dream.

Once she had found the raw space, Jo Ellin briefed Pierce Allen to create a "serene, tranquil haven," which would provide respite from the hectic pace of her international business life. She commissioned Pierce Allen to transform the existing two levels into the living, dining, and sleeping areas with plans to extend the space to a third level built onto the roof. As the proposed extension would affect the New York skyline, extensive work was required with the Landmark Commission to get the planning application approved. The application took a year to be processed, during which time

Right Random smudges of gold leaf soften the white-painted exposed brickwork. An antique chair, covered in rose-coloured velvet, dominates the muted elemental decor of the space. The monochromatic paintings were a present from Pierce Allen.

Pierce Allen recreated the proposed architectural profile as a series of wooden uprights connected with string on the roof and hired an aerial film crew to film the final outline. The approval was finally received for the scheme, and Jo Ellin proceeded, in conjunction with Pierce Allen, to construct, as she describes it, her "floating boat." The third level of space was to be used as a "chill-out zone" for the adults, also doubling as a crash pad for her numerous nieces and nephews.

Jo Ellin appointed Pierce Allen because "they knew my taste and would work with it, rather than impose their taste upon me." Jo Ellin describes her style as "cohesive eclecticism," founded on a series of individual pieces, often antiques, that each have a resonance for her. These pieces intermittently punctuate the lofty, high-ceilinged space, creating individual areas that are as much defined by their function as by the pieces themselves.

The triplex is entered on the middle level through a concealed central staircase, leading down to the sleeping and bathing areas on the level below on one side, and up to the roof extension on the other. The dining room, staircase, and the kitchen form part of the central block within the space, with two long window-

Above Left A rare wooden Japanese tea chest, here shown in detail, has been inset into a dividing wall. On one side it provides a focal point for the dining room; on the other side it leads the eye away from the semi-industrial overtones of the entrance hall.

Below Left The staircase leading up to the LA-style roof extension establishes a change of mood through its coral-pink painted walls, sisal floor covering, and porthole-style lighting.

filled hallways on either side leading to the open-plan living area. In order to balance the angularity of the interior architecture, Pierce Allen introduced curves and circular motifs into the furnishings.

The first antique piece that introduces this secondary circular theme – a round Japanese wooden tea chest – dominates both the hallway and the dining room on the other side of the wall on which it rests. Inset into a square cutout of the dividing wall, the tea chest forms a visual connection between both hallway and dining areas. The dining area is framed on two sides by internal walls, each constructed around key pieces of antique furniture. The wall opposite to that housing the tea chest has been built around an antique mahogany lawyer's chest, originally used to hold legal files. Jo Ellin has replaced hand-written legal notes with hand-cut crystal glassware and porcelain tableware. The second circular motif is the highly polished mahogany dining table, which serves as the main focal point of the room. Jo Ellin wanted a round table that could seat eight to ten people comfortably, because, as she explains, "a circular table fosters conversation." Generously proportioned carver chairs, covered in warm rich textural fabric, surround the

Right The elegant dining room has been created from the space between two parallel corridors. A huge brass "peach" covers the ceiling in a pattern of dots. Below, the mahogany table is surrounded by carver chairs, re-covered by DD Allen in a Donghia fabric.

table and give the room an inviting, luxurious atmosphere. Overhead, and continuing the circular motif, hangs a dramatic brass orb pendant light, which Jo Ellin describes as a "perforated brass peach." A find by DD Allen, the orb dapples the ceiling with light at night. The two open sides of the dining area open onto window-filled hallways, hung on either side with deep sage-green shot-silk taffeta drapes, lined in dusky rose-coloured brushed wool. When drawn, the drapes create an intimate, self-enclosed dining area, transforming the space into an almost secret enclave.

On the other side of the dining room, backing onto the staircase, is the open-plan kitchen and concealed galley storage area, opening out onto the window-filled lounge. White-painted, exposed brickwork walls reflect the natural daylight flooding the space and, on closer inspection, reveal random smudges of gold leaf applied directly onto the brickwork which intermittently catch the light. In order to diffuse some of the light and provide some privacy, the lower half of the windows are draped with an ecru loose-weave hessian-like fabric attached to a slackened tension wire, which creates a unique form of roman blind. Between the white,

low-slung, modern sofa and the matching armchair is a curved, sugar-pink, deep-buttoned velvet chair, which complements the dark wood coffee table and matching cabinet. The arrangement further exemplifies the Pierce Allen design philosophy of incorporating curves into the more linear areas. A stone fireplace with black hearth is decorated with two monochromatic abstract paintings, hung one above the other. Standing next to it is an antique wood-and-glass cabinet, housing all the implements necessary for mixing the perfect cocktail. As Jo Ellin

Above A dramatic Murano glass chandelier hangs in the master bedroom. A low-level wenge chest of drawers exhibits an almost transparent Murano table lamp. A pair of antique gilded chairs, upholstered in black silk moiré, anchor the space, while an inviting fawn velvet armchair fills a corner of the room.

Left The ensuite bathroom to the master bedroom is a successful "white on white" textural exercise. Glossy ceramic tiles line the walls, merging with marble floor tiles and the white-painted brick wall. An antique medicine cabinet houses towels and fragrances.

Above The back of the
antique Japanese tea chest
adds form and texture to
the entrance hall. In the
hallway, a 1950s Perspex
table holds a collection
of brightly coloured
contemporary glassware
and a flesh-toned high-
backed chair adds warmth
to the neutral palette.

explains, "I collect antique pieces that
I react strongly to… This piece that I use to
house bar accessories, including a
cocktail shaker, makes me feel like Myrna
Loy in a black-and-white movie. It conjures
up images for me of wafting in a satin
gown with fluffy slippers, pouring a drink
from a silver cocktail shaker."

The element of understated glamour
continues on the bedroom and bathroom
level below. The master bedroom,
designed as Jo Ellin's personal "haven,"
is a light, elegant, and serene space,
framed by walls of white backlit

diaphanous drapes hanging in front of
the windows on two sides. The room
is predominantly decorated with several
Italian antique pieces bought by Jo Ellin,
as they reminded her of her Italian
grandparents' home, and a highly
elaborate chandelier, sourced by DD
Allen in Paris. A dark walnut contemporary
cabinet holds an ornate, hand-blown,
sorbet-coloured Murano glass table lamp,
and is flanked by two Italian gilded antique
chairs upholstered in black silk velvet. A
large, cool grey, velvet armchair sits next
to a low occasional table holding a Danny
Lane glass vase. On the bed a luxurious,
tasselled cashmere throw refers back to
the cool tones of the armchair. Because
Jo Ellin wanted the room to have a
spacious and uncluttered ambience,
Pierce Allen designed a large walk-in
wardrobe next to the entrance to the
ensuite bathroom, so the bedroom could
be left as an elegant yet minimal space.

Designed by Michael Pierce, who
Jo Ellin describes as a "great bathroom
maker," the ensuite bathroom uses several
shades of white tile to create a textural,
glossy, and backlit "white on white" space,
with a generously proportioned
washstand, bath, and shower. The oval
silver mirror, wall-mounted over the double

sink, perfectly balances the antique chrome-and-glass medicine cabinet used to display bathroom accessories.

Pierce Allen used spot colour in varying degrees of scale and intensity in unexpected places throughout the space. Colour moves from the ethereal whiteness of the bathroom on the lower level to the stairwell, flooded in a shocking pink light that bounces off its bubblegum walls. The vibrantly coloured stairwell walls introduce the more casual LA/Miami-style rooftop "den," where neon-painted tongue-and-groove panelling and modular banquette seating literally shout "party time" from the rooftops of New York.

Framing the New York skyline like limited edition prints, the glass windows present a conservative exterior that belies the wild interior within. Galvanized steel chairs stand on giant square stone slabs like strategically placed pieces on a chessboard. A Panavision scene with the volume turned down, the New York urban soundtrack below becomes a muted sonic backdrop, while inside the sound of a cocktail being shaken fills this elegantly eclectic, erstwhile industrial, warehouse.

Below The elemental lines of the rooftop extension provide a natural frame for the panoramic New York skyline reflected in the glass panes. A series of galvanized chairs sit under the reflected cityscapes, like an audience in waiting.

Conclusion

The creation of a modern eclectic interior centres on designing your own personal blueprint, free from the diktats and tyranny of trends. It is not about a particular new shape, colour, or texture; it is about creating your own personal world in moving images, rather than a series of freeze frames. It is much more of a process, an exploration, rather than a predetermined design destination, focusing instead on making a personal journey. Using a form of artistic alchemy to meld internal and external influences, the creation of a modern eclectic interior combines several aesthetics, each driven by the passions and personality of its creator. The keynote is freedom of expression. The kind of freedom that independent creative thought brings to established forms of interior design manifests itself in the multisensory experience that is the modern eclectic interior.

In such an arena, individual identity, reflecting both personal and aspirational characteristics, is reinforced by the home environment, rather than the home itself being first to establish an external identity.

External environments in modern eclecticism provide a totally three-dimensional framework to support the inner lives of their creators. The ethos and atmosphere of a home based on modern eclecticism is established as much by things that one cannot buy as by the particular and often unusual objects that have a symbolic resonance for their owners. This added emotional response and connection with an environment gives the modern eclectic home a more personal layer, which is driven much more by unique passion than by fashion.

The creation of a modern eclectic environment is by no means a linear experience, but is equivalent to operating a joystick in an infinite design galaxy. The multilayered design process can be extremely complex as it can move backwards into bygone eras or forwards into futuristic phantasmagorical imaginings. It can be pushed sideways into other mediums or into neutral in order to access a more spiritual level. Whether driven by spontaneity or spatial quality, by cohesion or contradiction, modern eclecticism

Left The oak-panelled walls of this Georgian library establish a dark intimacy. A Philippe Starck lamp and a string of chilli lights illuminate the room. A striking, serenely smiling, statue from Quito in Equador is "a patron saint known to bring good luck."

Above Left The mini white fibreglass chair by Verner Panton, a perfect replica of the full-sized original, forms part of a "designer classics" collection that furnish a child's bedroom in Munich.

Above Centre The dark oak, 18th-century side table, part of a nest of tables, stands on blonde woodstrip flooring. On the table a tall, brushed aluminium vase with dark undulating horizontal lines.

Above Right The spiralling flame-coloured porcelain vase, fading to white on its fluted neck, is a retro piece found in a flea market in Pfaffelhofen on the outskirts of Munich. It provides a spot of intense colour to the dark walnut dining table below.

Below Left A late 1960s chair, upholstered in truffle brown corduroy, almost seems to float on its transparent Perspex base, shown here in detail. A "no name" one-off, the chair was found in a local flea market in Germany.

Below Centre This zebra-skin forms the floor-level focal point on an otherwise fairly traditional parquet flooring. Its graphic quality gives an immediate retro feel.

Below Right The ornate detailing of a gilded gesso 18th-century English table, now residing in an apartment in New York, is juxtaposed with the matt lemon-yellow perforated panels that box in radiators under the window.

Below A giant cast concrete cog, part of a sculptural piece, is held up by a tall iron plinth. With inherent industrial and historical references, the piece connects the industrial heritage of the space with the medieval elements of the furnishings.

will always be an "off road experience." In modern eclecticism a home interior centres on the creation of a series of satellites. Individual, often independent, environments are informed by a cast of personal characteristics, which are connected via often-intangible elements, frequently apparent only to their creators. The degree of importance may vary for each area, determined by the amount of time spent in each space and whether its use is predominantly as a public or private zone.

By "adjusting the volume," so to speak, eclecticism is a philosophy that can be shouted or whispered, and often fluctuates between the two. The eclectic form of this creative process can be likened to laying down a track of music by first composing the notes, which then evolve into a theme tune, which is further punctuated by a percussion section. Veering from adagio to andante to crescendo, the eclectic interior is built up layer by layer until it becomes the "surround

sound" equivalent of a fully blown symphony. The visual thread that determines the interior can then be deconstructed into a series of individual elements or reconstructed to form a new "melody." This in turn can be interpreted and expressed in different forms, as if playing the signature theme tune first as a piano sonata through to a three-act opera via echoes of modern jazz to rock and back again.

Modern eclecticism is about personal style and creative self-expression. Not only this, it is about doing your own edit without boundaries – a form of design improvisation that is free from the confines of the autocue form of interior design. The modern eclectic home is the ultimate form of individual self-expression: the public face of expressing the personal. Centring on making the personal visible, it is a high-octane form of a personal statement in three-dimensional form, borne of a celebration of the diversity of our world.

Above These African carvings, found by the owners during their first trip to Kenya, are appropriately entitled "The Kiss." Made by local tribes' people and hand-carved with exquisite detailing, they now inhabit a wall-mounted floating glass shelf in London.

Directory

General Advice

The American Institute of Architects
1735 New York Avenue NW
Washington DC 20006-5292
USA
Tel: +1 202 626 7300
Fax: +1 202 626 7426
www.aiaonline.com

Association of Licensed Architects
PO Box 687
Barrington IL 60011-0687
USA
Tel: +1 847 382 0630
Fax: +1 847 382 8380
email: AssocLicArch@aol.com
www.licensedarchitect.org

Canadian Home Builders Association
150 Laurier Avenue West
Suite 200
Ottawa
Ontario K1P5J4
Canada
Tel: +1 613 230 3060
Fax: +1 613 232 8214
www.chba@chba.ca

Federation of Master Builders
Gordon Fisher House
14-15 Great James Street
London WC1N 3DP
UK
Tel: +44 (0)20 7242 7583
Fax: +44 (0)20 7404 0296
email: central@fmb.org.uk
www.fmb.org.uk

Fédération Nationale du Batiment
33 Avenue Kléber
75016 Paris
France
Tel: +33 1 4069 5100
Fax: +33 1 4553 5877

Interior Decorators and Designers Association
London SW10 OXE
Tel: +44 (0)20 7349 0800
www.idda.co.uk

National Association of Home Builders
1201 15th Street, NW
Washington DC 20005
USA
Tel: +1 800 368 5242
email: info@NHAB.com
www.nahb.com

National Association of Plumbing, Heating and Mechanical Services
14-15 Ensign House
Ensign Business Centre
Westwood Way
Coventry CV4 8JA
UK
Tel: +44 (0)20 7647 0626

Painting and Decorating Federation
Construction House
Leonard Street
London EC2A 4JX
UK
Tel: +44 (0)20 7608 5093

Royal Institute of British Architects
66 Portland Place
London W1B 1AD
UK
Tel: +44 (0)20 7580 5533
Fax: +44 (0)20 7255 1541
www.architecture.com

Royal Institute of Chartered Surveyors
12 Great George Street
London SW1P 3AD
UK
Tel: +44 (0)20 7222 7000
www.rics.org

Paint

Alto Country Colour
8 Railway Street
Newmarket
New Zealand
Tel: +64 9 522 2019

Crown Paints
Crown House
PO Box 37
Hollins Road
Darwen
Lancashire BB3 0BG
UK
Tel: +44 (0)1254 704 951
www.crownpaint.co.uk

Designers Guild
Head Office
3 Olaf Street
London W11 4BE
UK
Tel: +44 (0)20 7243 7300
Fax: +44 (0)20 7243 7320
www.designersguild.com

Dulux Advice Centre
Wexham Road
Slough
Berkshire SL2 5DS
UK
Tel: +44 (0)1753 550 555
www.dulux.co.uk

Hammerite Products Ltd
Prudhoe
Northumberland NE24 6LP
UK
Tel: +44 (0)1661 8300 000
www.hammerite.com

L Cornelissen and Son Ltd
105 Great Russell Street
London WC1B 3RY
UK
Tel: +44 (0)20 7636 1045
Fax: +44 (0)20 7636 3655
email: info@cornelissen.com

The Old Fashioned Milk Paint Co
436 Main Street
PO Box 222
Groton MA 01450
USA
Tel: +1 978 448 6336

Auro Organic Paints
Sinan Company
PO Box 856
2202 Muir Woods Place
Davis CA 95617
USA
Tel: +1 916 753 3104

Paint and Paper Library
5 Elystan Street
London SW3 3NT
UK
Tel: +44 (0)20 7823 7755
Fax: +44 (0)20 7823 7766
www.paintlibrary.co.uk

Papers and Paints Ltd
4 Park Walk
Chelsea
London SW10 0AD
UK
Tel: +44 (0)20 7352 8626

Pittsburgh Paints
PPG Industries
1 PPG Place
Pittsburgh PA 15272
USA
Tel: +1 888 774 1010

Wallcoverings

Brian Yates
G27 Chelsea Harbour Design Centre
Chelsea Harbour
London SW10 OXE
Tel: +44 (0)20 7352 0123
Fax: +44 (0)20 7352 6060
email: sales@brian-yates.co.uk

Crown Wallpapers
88 Ronson Drive
Rexdale
Ontario M9W 1B9
Canada
Tel: +1 416 245 2900

Designers Guild
(See Paint)

Donghia UK Ltd
23 The Design Centre
Chelsea Harbour
London SW10 OXE
UK
Tel: +44 (0)20 7823 3456
Fax: +44 (0)20 7376 5758

Hamilton Weston Wallpapers
Classic Revivals Inc
1 Design Center Place
Suite 545
Boston MA 02210
USA
Tel: +1 617 574 9030

Muraspec
74-78 Wood Lane End
Hemel Hempstead
Hertfordshire HP2 4RF
UK
Tel: +44 (0)8705 117 118

Ornamenta
3/12 The Design Centre
Chelsea Harbour
London SW10 0XE
UK
Tel: +44 (0)20 7352 1824
Fax: +44 (0)20 7376 3398
www.ornamenta.co.uk

Osborne & Little
304 King's Road
London SW3 5UH
UK
Tel: +44 (0)20 7352 1456
www.osborneandlittle.com

Tektura plc
Head Office
One Heron Quay
Docklands
London E14 4JA
UK
Tel: +44 (0)20 7536 3300
Fax: +44 (0)20 7536 3322
www.tektura.com

Fabric

Baumann Fabrics
114 North Centre Avenue
Rockville
Rockville Centre
New York NY 11570
USA
Tel:+1 516 7647431

Designers Guild
(See Paint)

J Robert Scott UK Inc
Unit 19, Second Floor
Chelsea Harbour Design Centre
London SW10 0XE
UK
Tel: +44 (0)20 7376 4705
Fax: +44 (0)20 7376 4706

NYA Nordiska Textiles
2/26 Chelsea Harbour Design Centre
Chelsea Harbour
London SW10 0XE
UK
Tel: +44 (0)20 7351 2783
Fax: +44 (0)20 7352 5305
www.nya-nordiska.com

Sahco Hesslein
24 Chelsea Harbour Design Centre
Chelsea Harbour
London SW10 0XE
UK
Tel: +44 (0)20 7352 6168
Fax: +44 (0)20 7352 0767
email: london@sahco-hesslein.com
www.sahco-hesslein.com

Scalamandré Silks
300 Trade Zone Drive
Ronkonkoma
New York NY 22779-7381
USA
Tel: +1 516 467 8800

Squigee
58 Fox Street
Second Floor
Glasgow G1 4AU
UK
Tel: +44 (0)141 400 3151
Fax: +44 (0)141 400 3150
email: info@squigee.com
www.squigee.com

Zimmer+Rohde UK Ltd
15 Chelsea Harbour Design Centre
London SW10 0XE
UK
Tel: +44 (0)20 7351 7115
Fax: +44 (0)20 7351 5661
email: zimmer@z-r.co.uk
www.zimmer-rohde.com

Lighting

Babylon Design Ltd
301 Fulham Road
London SW10 9QH
UK
Tel: +44 (0)20 7376 7233

Catalytico
25 Montpelier Street
London SW7 1HF
UK
Tel: +44 (0)20 7225 1720
Fax: +44 (0)20 7225 3740
email: catalyt@dircon.co.uk

Christopher Wray Lighting
591-593 Kings Road
London SW6 2YW
UK
Tel: +44 (0)20 7751 8701
www.christopherwray.com

Colour Light Co Ltd
Unit 28
Riverside Business Centre
Victoria Street
High Wycombe
Bucks HP11 2LT
Tel: +44 (0)1494 462112
Fax: +44 (0)1494 462612
email: jeremylord@cix.co.uk

Kreon nv
Frankrijklei 112
2000 Antwerpen
Belgium
Tel: +32 3231 2422
Fax: +32 3231 8896
email: mailbox@kreon.be
www.kreon.be

Luceplan USA Inc
315 Hudson Street
NY 10013
USA
Tel: +1 212 989 6265
Fax: +1 212 462 4349
email: info@luceplanusa.com
www.luceplanusa.com

Minx Design
67 Great Western Studios
Great Western Road
London W9 3NY
Tel: +44 (0)20 7289 5621
email: info@minxdesign.net
www.minxdesign.net

Modular Lighting Instruments
Rumbeeksesteenweg 258-260
8800 Roeselare
Belgium
Tel: +32 5126 5656
Fax: +32 5122 8004
email: welcome@supermodular.com
www.supermodular.com

Nelson
PO Box 17357
London SW9 0WB
UK
Tel: +44 (0)20 8519 8694
www.julienelson.co.uk

Flooring

All State Rubber Co
105-12
101st Avenue
Ozone Park NY 11416
USA
Tel +1 718 526 7890

Alma Leather Ltd
Unit D
12-14 Greatorex Street
London E1 5NF
UK
Tel: +44 (0)20 7375 0343
Fax: +44 (0)20 7375 2471

Amtico Co
Kingfield Road
Coventry CV6 5AA
UK
Tel: +44 024 7686 1400
www.amtico.com

Bill Amberg
10 Chepstow Road
London W2 5BD
UK
Tel: +44 (0)20 7727 3560
Fax: +44 (0)20 7727 3541
www.billamberg.com

Bonar Floors Ltd (UK)
High Holborn Road
Ripley
Derby DE5 3NT
UK
Tel: +44 (0)1773 744 121
www.bonarfloors.com

Bonar Floors Ltd (US)
USA Sales Department
Tel: +1 770 252 4890
Fax: +1 770 252 4894
www.bonarfloors.com

Country Floors
15 East 16th Street
New York NY 10003
USA
Tel: +1 212 6278300

Dalsouple
PO Box 140
Bridgwater
Somerset TA5 1HT
UK
Tel: +44 01984 66 75 51
email: info@dalsouple.com
www.dalsouple.com

Fired Earth
Twyford Mill
Oxford Road
Adderbury
Oxfordshire OX17 3HP
UK
Tel: +44 (0)1295 812 088
www.firedearth.com

Forbo Nairn
PO Box 1
Kirkcaldy
Fife KY1 2SB
Scotland
Tel: +44 (0)1592 6472 09
www.marmoleum.co.uk

Hardwood Flooring Co Ltd
146 West End Lane
London NW6 1SD
UK
Tel: +44 (0)20 7328 8481
Fax: +44 (0)20 7625 5951
www.hardwood-flooring.uk.com

Kahrs UK Ltd
Unit 2 West
68 Bognor Road
Chichester
West Sussex PO19 2NS
UK
Tel: +44 (0)1243 778 747
Fax: +44 (0)1243 531 237
www.kahrs.se

Kirkstone
Skelwith Bridge
Nr Ambleside
Cumbria LA22 9NN
UK
Tel: +44 (0)1539 433 296

LASSCO Flooring
41 Maltby Street
London SE1 3PA
UK
Tel: +44 (0)20 7237 4488
email: flooring@lassco.co.uk
www.lassco.co.uk

Mannington Wood Floors
Mannington Mills Inc
1327 Lincoln Drive
High Pond NC 27260
USA
Tel: +1 800 252 4202

Mosaik Pierre Mesguich Ltd
10 Kensington Square
London W8 5EP
UK
Tel: +44 (0)20 7795 6253
email: info@mosaik.demon.co.uk

Natural Flooring Direct
46 Webbs Road
Battersea
London SW11 6SF
UK
Tel: +44 0800 454 721
www.reeveflooring.co.uk

Paris Ceramics Ltd
583 King's Road
London SW6 2EH
UK
Tel: +44 (0)20 7371 7778
Fax: +44 (0)20 7371 8395
www.parisceramics.com

Perucchetti Associates
15 Townmead Road
London SW6 2QL
Tel: +44 (0)20 7371 5497
Fax: +44 (0)20 7371 5842
email: office@perucchetti.com

Solid Floor
53 Pembridge Road
London W11 3HG
UK
Tel: +44 (0)20 7221 9166
www.solidfloor.co.uk

Stone Age Ltd
19 Filmer Road
London SW6 7BU
Tel: +44 (0)20 7385 7954
Fax: +44 (0)20 7385 7956
www.estone.co.uk

Furniture and Accessories

Alma Leather Ltd
(See Flooring)

Anna Chron
Tor Str
Mitte
10119 Berlin
Germany
Tel: +49 30 4404 6514
www.annachron.de

AREA ID Moderne
262 Elizabeth Street
(Between Houston and
Prince Street)
New York
10012 NY
USA
Tel: +1 212 219 9903
www.areaid.net

Aspectos
C/Rec 28
08003 Barcelona
Spain
Tel: +34 93 319 5285

B&B Italia
Strada Provinciale, 32
22060 Novedrate (COMO)
Italy
Tel: +39 031 795 213
Fax: +39 031 795 224
email: beb@bebitalia.it
www.bebitalia.it

BD Ediciones de Diseño
C/Mallorca 291
Barcelona
Spain
Tel: +34 93 458 6909
www.bdbarcelona.com

BD Ediciones de Diseño
C/Villanueva 5
28001 Madrid
Spain
Tel: +34 91 435 0627
www.bdmadrid.com

**Birdman Furniture
and Kate Hume Glass**
Sales and Press enquiries
Netherlands
Tel: +31 (0)20 625 3522
Fax: +31 (0)20 420 5750
email: mail@birdmanfurniture
email: kate.hume@euronet.nl
www.birdmanfurniture.com

Boutique Eileen
Georgenstrasse 70
80799 Munich
Germany
Tel: +49 89 27 77 40 60
Fax: +49 89 27 77 40 61
email: boutique.eileen@topmail.de

Catherine Memmi
34 rue St-Sulpice
75006 Paris
France
Tel: +33 1 4407 2228
Fax: +33 1 4407 2227

Century Design
68 Marylebone High Street
London W1U 5JH
UK
Tel: +44 (0)20 7487 5100

The Conran Shop
Michelin House
81 Fulham Road
London SW3 6RD
UK
Tel: +44 (0)20 7589 7401
www.conran.com

Dadriade
Rosenthaler Strasse 40-41
Mitte
10178 Berlin
Germany
Tel: +49 30 2852 8720

David Gill Gallery
60 Fulham Road
London SW3
UK
Tel: +44 (0)20 7589 5946

De Kasstoor
Rozengracht 202-210
1016 NC Amsterdam
Netherlands
Tel: +31 (0)20 521 8112
Fax: +31 (0)20 521 8111

Egg
36 Kinnerton Street
London SW1X 8ES
UK
Tel: +44 (0)20 7235 9315
Fax: +44 (0)20 7838 9705

European Design Centre
Kenilworth House
79-80 Margaret Street
London W1W 82A
UK
Tel: +44 (0)20 7255 2524
email: sales@edcplc.com
www.edcplc.com

The Frozen Fountain
Prinsengracht 629-645
1016 HV Amsterdam
Netherlands
Tel: +31 (0)20 622 9375

Galerie Jochum and Tissi
Alte Schönhauser Strasse 38
Mitte
10119 Berlin
Germany
Tel: +49 30 247 247 14
Fax: +49 30 247 247 94
email: jochumtissi@snafu.de
www.jochumtissi.de

Galerie KIS
Paleisstraat 107
1012 ZL Amsterdam
Netherlands
Tel: +31 (0)20 620 9760

Glasgalerie Kuhler
Prinsengracht 134
1015 EB Amsterdam
Netherlands
Tel: +31 (0)20 638 0230

Galerie Weinand
Oranienplatz 5
Kreuzberg
10999 Berlin
Germany
Tel: +49 30 614 2545
email: weinand.galerie@snafu.de

Gotham
C/Cervantes 7
Barrio Gotico
Barcelona
Spain
Tel: +34 93 412 4647

Heal's
196 Tottenham Court Road
London W1P 7LQ
UK
Tel: +44 (0)20 7636 1666
www.heals.co.uk

The Holding Company
241-5 King's Road
London SW3 5EL
UK
Tel: +44 (0)20 7352 1600
www.theholdingcompay.co.uk

Knoll
1235 Water Street
East Greenville
18041 PA
USA
www.knoll.com

Kunsthandel frans leidelmeijer
Nieuwe spiegelstraat 58
1017 DH Amsterdam
Netherlands
Tel: +31 (0)20 625 4627
email: frans@leidelmeijer.nl
www.leidelmeijer.nl

Ligne Roset
23-25 Mortimer Street
London W1T 3JE
UK
Tel: +44 (0)20 7323 1248
Fax: +44 (0)20 7323 1247
www.ligne-roset-london.co.uk

Limn
290 Townsend Street
San Francisco
USA
Tel: +1 415 543 5466
www.limn.com

Malin Iovino Design
43 St Saviours Wharf
Mill Street
London SE1 2BE
UK
Tel/Fax: +44 (0)20 7252 3542
Mob: 079956 326122
email: iovino@btinternet.com

Mission
45 Hereford Road
London W2 5AH
UK
Tel: +44 (0)20 7792 4633
Fax: +44 (0)20 7229 9891

Muji
41 Carnaby Street
London W1V 1PD
UK
Tel: +44 (0)20 7287 7323
Fax: +44 (0)20 7287 6987
email: mujicarnaby@aol.com

Muriel Grateau
130 Galerie de Valois
Jardins du Palais Royal
Paris 75001
France
Tel: +33 1 4020 9030
Fax: +33 1 4296 1232

Poliform
Via Montesanto, 28
22044 Inverigo (CO)
Italy
Tel: +39 0316 951
Fax: +39 0316 994 44
www.poliform.it

Porro srl
Via per Cant – 35
22060 Montesolaro (CO)
Italy
Tel: +39 031 780 237
Fax: +39 031 781 529
email: info@porro.com
www.porro.com

Pure Living
Ground Floor
1-3 Leonard Street
London EC2A 4AQ
UK
Tel: +44 (0)20 7250 1116
Fax: +44 (0)20 7250 0616
email: mail@puredesignuk.com

SCP
135-139 Curtain Road
London EC2A 3BX
UK
Tel: +44 (0)20 7739 1869
Fax: +44 (0)20 7729 4224
www.scp.co.uk

Sentou
26 bd Raspail 7th
Paris
France
Tel: +33 1 4549 0005

Space
214 Westbourne Grove
London W11 2RH
UK
Tel: +44 (0)20 7229 6533
Fax: +44 (0)20 7727 0134
email: space@spaceshop.co.uk

Studio B Home
334 King Street East, Suite 100
Toronto
Ontario M5A 1K3
Canada
Tel: +1 416 363 2996
Fax: +1 416 363 2997
www.studiobhome.com

Succession
179 Westbourne Grove
London W11 2SB
UK
Tel: +44 (0)20 7727 0580
Fax: +44 (0)20 7229 2588

Themes and Variations
231 Westbourne Grove
London W11 2SE
UK
Tel: +44 (0)20 7727 5531
Fax: +44 (0)20 7221 6378
email: go@themesandvariations.co.uk

Tom Tom
42 New Compton Street
London WC2H 8DA
UK
Tel/Fax: +44 (0)20 7240 7909
email: sales@tomtomshop.co.uk
www.tomtomshop.co.uk

Totem Design
71 Franklin Street
(Between Broadway and Church
Street)
New York
USA
Tel: +1 212 925 5506

Twentytwentyone
274 Upper Street
London N1 2UA
UK
Tel: +44 (0)20 7288 1996
www.twentytwentyone.com

Vitra Ltd
30 Clerkenwell Road
London EC1
UK
Tel: +44 (0)20 7608 6200
Fax: +44 (0)20 7608 6201
email: info_uk@vitra.com
www.vitra.com

Kitchens

Aga Cookers Inc
RFD 1
Box 477
Stowe VT 05672
USA
Tel: +1 802 253 9727

ALNO (UK) Ltd
Unit 10
Hampton Farm Industrial Estate
Hampton Road West
Hanworth
Middlesex TW13 6DB
UK
Tel: +44 (0)20 8898 4781
Fax: +44 (0)20 8898 0268
email: alno@aol.com
www.alnouk.co.uk

Kitchen Aid
2000 M-63
Mail Drop 4302
Benton Harbour MI 49022
USA
Tel: +1 800 253 3977

Miele Co Ltd
Fairacres
Marcham Road
Abingdon
Oxon OX14 1TW
UK
Tel: +44 (0)1235 554 455
www.meile.co.uk

SieMatic Corporation
Two Greenwood Square
331 Street Road
Suite 450
Bensalem PA 19020
USA
Tel: +1 215 244 6800

Siemens
Grand Union House
Old Wolverton Road
Wolverton
Milton Keynes MK12 5PT
UK
Tel: +44 (0)1908 328 400
www.siemensappliances.co.uk

Smeg (UK) Limited
87 A Milton Park
Abingdon
Oxon OX14 4RY
UK
Tel/Brochure: +44 (0)8708 437 373
Fax: +44 (0)1235 861 120
www.smeguk.com

Strato Kitchens
Via Piemonte 9
23018 Talamona (SO)
Italy
Tel: +39 0342 610869
Fax: +39 0342 610418
email: strato@stratocucine.com

Subtle
16 Hewett Street
Shoreditch
London EC2A 3NN
UK
Tel: +44 (0)8707 459 003
Fax: +44 (0)8707 459 004
www.subtleinteriors.com

Zanussi
55-77 High Street
Slough
Berkshire SL1 1DZ
UK
Tel: +44 (0)8705 727 727
www.zanussi.co.uk

Bathrooms

Armitage Shanks Ltd
Armitage
Rugeley
Staffs WS15 4BT
Tel: +44 (0)1543 490 253
Fax: +44 (0)1543 491 677

Aston Matthews Ltd
141-147A Essex Road
Islington
London N1 2SN
Tel: +44 (0)20 7226 7220
Fax: +44 (0)20 7354 5951
www.astonmatthews.co.uk

CP Hart
Newnham Terrace
Hercules Road
London SE1 7DR
Tel/Fax: +44 (0)20 7902 1000
www.cphart.co.uk

Hansgrohe
Units D1 and D2
Sandown Park Trading Estate
Royal Mills
Esher
Surrey KT10 8BL
Tel: +44 (0)1372 465 655
Email: sales@hansgrohe.co.uk
Email: info@hansgrohe.co.uk
www.hansgrohe.co.uk

Hastings Bath Collection
30 Commercial Street
Freeport NY 11520
USA
Tel: +1 216 379 3500

LASSCO RBK
Britannia Walk
London
N1 7LU
Tel: +44 (0)20 7366 822

Lasco Bathware
3255 East Miraloma Avenue
Anaheim CA 92806
USA
Tel: +1 800 877 0464
www.lascobathware.com

Submarine
8 Lanark Street
Glasgow G1 5PY
Tel: +44 (0)141 564 9867
Fax: +44 (0)141 243 2424
www.submarinedesign.co.uk

Villeroy and Boch (UK) Ltd
267 Merton Road
London SW18 5JS
Tel: +44 (0)20 8871 4028
www.villeroy-boch.com

Vintage Plumbing and Bathroom Antiques
9645 Sylvia Avenue
Northridge CA 91324
USA
Tel: +1 818 772 1721

Architects and Designers

Architectus Bowes Clifford Thomson Ltd
PO Box 90621 AMSC
Auckland
New Zealand
Tel: +64 9 307 5970
Fax: +64 9 307 5972
www.architectus.co.nz

Arthur Collin Architect
1a Berry Place
London EC1V 0JD
UK
Tel: +44 (0)20 7490 3520
Fax: +44 20 7490 3521
email: info@arthurcollin.com
www.arthurcollin.com

Belmont Freeman Architects
110 West 40th Street, suite 2401
New York
NY 10018
USA
Tel: +1 212 382 3311
Fax: +1 212 730 1229
www.belmontfreeman.com

Claesson Koivisto Rune Architects
Sankt Paulsgatan 25
S-11848 Stockholm
Sweden
Tel: +46 8 644 5863
Fax: +46 8 644 5883
email: arkitektkontor@claesson-koivisto-rune.se

Clare Design
41 McLaren Street
North Sydney
New South Wales 2060
Australia
Tel: +61 2 9929 0072
Fax: +61 2 9959 5765
email: claredesign@tmg.com.au

Claudio Silvestrin Architects Ltd
Unit 18 Waterside
44 - 48 Wharf Road
London N1 7UX
Tel: +44 (0)20 7490 7797
Fax: +44 (0)20 7490 7272
www.claudiosilvestrin.com

D'Soto Architects
38 Mount Pleasant
London WC1X 0AP
UK
Tel: +44 (0)20 7278 5100
email: info@dosto.com

David Chipperfield
1a Cobham Mews
Agar Grove
London NW1 9SB
UK
Tel: +44 (0)20 7267 9422

Deborah Berke Architect
211 West 19th Street, 2nd Floor
New York
NY 10011
USA
Tel: +1 212 229 9211
Fax: +1 212 989 3347
www.dberke.com

Edge (HK) Ltd
Room 1706-08
663 King's Road,
North Point
Hong Kong
Tel: +852 2802 6212
Fax: +852 2802 6213
email: edgeltd@netvigator.com
www.edge.hk.com

Engelen Moore
44 McLachlan Avenue
Rushcutters bay
Sydney
New South Wales 2011
Australia
Tel: +61 2 9380 4099
Fax: +61 2 9380 4302
email: architects@engelen
moore.com.au
www.engelenmoore.com.au

Entasis Arkitekter
Sankt Peder Straede 34a
2nd floor
1453 Copenhagen K
Denmark
Tel: +45 33 339 525

Escher GuneWardena
2404 Wilshire Blvd
Suite 502
Los Angeles
California CA 90057
USA
Tel: +1 213 413 2325
Fax: +1 213 413 7058
email: egarch@aol.com

Geistlweg-architektur
A-5411 Oberalm 441
Salzberg
Austria
Tel/Fax: +43 6245 81478
email: geistlwegarch@aon.at

Gluckman Mayner Architects
150 Hudson Street
New York
NY 10013
USA
Tel: +1 212 929 0100
Fax: +1 212 929 0833
www.gluckmanmayner.com

Hanrahan Meyers Architects
22 West 21st Street, room 1201
New York
NY 10010
USA
Tel: +1 212 989 6026
Fax: +1 212 255 3776

Jarmund Hansgrohe
Units D1 and D2
Sandown Park Trading estate
Royal Mills
Esher
Surrey KT10 8BL
Tel: +44 (0)1372 465 655
email: sales@hansgrohe.co.uk
email: info@hansgrohe.co.uk
www.hansgrohe.co.uk

Morris Sato Studio
219 East 12th Street, 1st Floor
New York
NY 10003
USA
Tel: +1 212 228 2832
Fax: +1 212 505 6160
email: MorrisSato@aol.com

Mark Guard Ltd Architects
161 Whitfield Street
London W1P 5RY
UK
Tel: +44 (0)20 7380 1199
Fax: +44 (0)20 7387 5441
email: mga@markguard.com

Níall McLaughlin
39-51 Highgate Road
London NW5 1RS
UK
Tel: +44 (0)20 7485 9170
Fax: +44 (0)20 7485 9171
www.niallmclaughlin.com

Vigsnäs
Kristian Augusts Gate 11
0164 Oslo
Norway
Tel: +47 2299 4343

**Pasanella and Klein, Stolzman
and Berg Architects**
330 West 42nd Street
New York
NY 10036
USA
Tel: +1 212 594 2010
Fax: +1 212 947 4381
www.pksb.com

Paxton Locher Architects
10 St Georges Mews
London NW1 8XE
UK
Tel: +44 (0)20 7586 6161
Fax: +44 (0)20 7586 7171
email:
mail@paxtonlocherarchitects.com

Pure Living
(See Furniture and Accessories)

RCR Aranda Pigem Vialta
Passeig de Blay 34
17800 Olot
Girona
Spain
Tel: +34 972 26 9105

Resolution: 4 Architecture
150 West 28th Street Suite 1902
New York
NY 10001
USA
Tel: +1 212 675 9266
Fax: +1 212 206 0944
email: jtanney@re4a.com
www.re4a.com

Rick Mather Architects
123 Camden High Street
London NW1 7JR
Tel: +44 (0)20 7284 1727
Fax: +44 (0)20 7267 7826
email: info@rickmather.com
www.rickmather.com

Rihl
63 Cross Street
London N1 2BB
UK
Tel: +44 (0)20 7704 6003
Fax: +44 (0)20 7688 0478
email: info@procter-rihl.com
www.procter-rihl.com

Seth Stein Architects
52 Kelso Place
London W8 5QQ
UK
Tel: +44 (0)20 7376 0005
email: admin@sethstein.com
www.sethstein.com

Smith-Miller and Hawkinson
305 Canal Street
New York
NY 10013
USA
Tel: +1 212 966 3875
Fax: +1 212 966 3877

Spencer Fung
3 Pine Mews
London NW10 3JA
UK
Tel: +44 (0)20 8960 9883

Stéphane Beel
Koningin Astridiaan 7/19
8200 Bruges
Belgium
Tel: +32 50 30 19 50
Fax: +32 50 39 18 97

Stephen Varady Architecture
14 Lackey Street
St Peters
New South Wales 2044
Australia
Tel: +61 2 9516 4044
Fax: +61 2 9516 4541

Studio Archea
Via della Fornace 30/R
50125 Florence
Italy
Tel: +39 055 688 097
email: staff@archea.it

UT Architecture
158 Lafayette Street
2nd Floor
New York 10013
USA
Tel: +1 212 966 8815
www.utarchitecture.com

Vicente Wolf Associates Inc
333 West 39th Street
New York
NY 10018
USA
Tel: +1 212 465 0590
Fax: +1 212 465 0639

**Winka Dubbeldam/
Archi-tectonics**
111 Mercer Street, 2nd Floor
New York
NY 10012
USA
Tel: +1 212 226 0303
email: winka@archi-tectonics.com

USEFUL WEBSITES

www.interiorinternet.com

www.furniture.com

www.lampa.com

www.totemdesign.com

www.industrial-home.com

www.chdc.co.uk
(Chelsea Design Centre)

Index

Acknowledgments

I would like to thank everyone we have featured in this book, in particular Patrice and Iza, Jac and Steve, Pierre and Kamilla, Kate and Franz, Carolin and Robert Stephan, Richard and Ree, Jo Ellin Comerford, Naomi and Oliver, Marguerite Marie Carlhian, and Joe Holzman – many of whom have since become friends – for allowing us into their homes and letting us dip into their lives for a little while and above all for making us feel so welcome while we were there. I would like to offer my personal thanks to Michael for his ability to turn any subject into an art form through his unique form of photography, which has given this book a visual dynamism I feel fortunate to be able to share. To everyone at our publishers, Mitchell Beazley, who worked so hard to help us realize this book in the exact form that we strived for, especially Lara and Auberon for sharing in our vision. To Katie who simplifies the complex, makes global travel run smoothly, and lends to everything and everyone she deals with an air of cool, calm intelligence – thank you for all your hard work and assistance in putting this book together. To my family for their total love and support and for showing me that everything is possible, also for their encouragement in those moments when I wasn't always quite sure. Finally, and most importantly, to my main men, all my love and thanks for always being there and for allowing me not always to be there enough, thank you for making me happier than I could ever have imagined possible – this book is for you.